Like a Vapor

LIFE IS TOO SHORT TO LIVE A LIE

Jamie Massey

FOREWORD BY
Perry and Pam Stone

Table of Contents

THE LIE

THE TRUTH

Acknowledgements

This book took years for me to experience and years to pen. God sent many people to confirm to me the call to write this book. However, countless times I would begin and find myself too broken to finish. Therefore, to all the many friends and family members who encouraged me and prayed for me through this process I say, Thank you.

To my precious husband, Victor who is still my knight in shining armor—thank you for understanding, undergirding, and believing in me. I love you so much, honey.

To my anointed sons, Micah and Caleb, you are still the best gifts that God ever gave to me. It's an honor to be your mother.

To my beautiful sisters, Shannon, Tonya, and Myla—thank you for allowing me to be open and transparent; to just be me. We have stood together through much and I'm so grateful to have you in my life. *Nothin' like sisters!*

To my extended family members, the Massey's and the Jeter's; thank you for being a support to me throughout the years. My life has been enriched because of you.

To Life Church International; thank you for your love and strength. You wouldn't let me quit.

To the many who did research and helped in the office, thank you for the assistance.

To Birdie Courtright who helped me tremendously in putting my thoughts on paper, thank you!

To the Lord Jesus Christ—Your amazing grace! I'm speechless! To You be all glory and honor and power and dominion! Thank you is just not enough...

Finally, I wish to dedicate this book to James and Mary Ann Jeter, my parents. Thank you Lord for everything you taught me through their lives—truths that still speak to me today.

Foreword

Perry and I have personally known Victor and Jamie Massey since we were young couples, on fire for God with the desire to transform lives through the preaching of the Gospel. Through the years our mutual vision of transforming lives has not changed. God molds our lives through numerous personal trials, tests, and faith stretching moments. Our seasons of allowing God to mold us have sharpened the sword of the Spirit that we wield today, preparing us to minister truth as the Lord brings us through our own tribulations. The book you are about to read was birthed through many long seasons of tribulation and testing.

Jamie is not only a wonderful wife and mother but she has distinguished herself as an anointed speaker and a gifted communicator. Her personal tragedies and tests in life have given her a first hand look at how the enemy operates—and what a believer must do when you find yourself in the middle of a difficult war with the enemy of your soul.

It is one thing for a person to preach a message that has inspired them. It is certainly another thing to hear from someone who has walked through the fire victoriously. Jamie has traveled dark paths, only to discover life sustaining light. She can look you in the eye and say with certainty, "I know what you're going through." This book, *Like A Vapor: Life Is Too Short To Live A Lie,* is the testimony of how God molded her—through tragedy, abuse and emotional breakdown. It will be an inspiration and a faith builder to all who read it.

Pam and Perry Stone

Preface

It has been said that perception is reality. The way we perceive our environment greatly affects the quality of our life as we make choices that chart our course. How true this is when it comes to my story. My sisters and I have memories of events, some different and some the same, that have lingered with us through the years and meshed to form who we are today. The story you are about to read is my recollection of some traumatizing and dramatic events. I want to share with you how these circumstances influenced my life.

Growing up, my father often quoted a scripture found in James 4:14:

"Whereas you do not know what will happen tomorrow. For what is your life? It is even a vapor that appears for a little time and then vanishes away."

After quoting the verse he always followed with a short and predictable sermon on the importance of not wasting your life. He reminded us not to open the door to the enemy because life was too short to live it for anyone other than God. This message stayed with me through the years and had much to do with the way I chose to live each day.

Friend, it is my prayer that after reading my story you too will choose to live your life for God. It is in Him we live, move, and have our being (Acts 17:28). Our very reason for existence and the purposes for which He created us are ours to discover in Him.

As you read the following pages you may find circumstances that you can relate to and identify with while other parts of my story might seem foreign or strange to you. I lived through the details that I'm sharing with you and I know there are others like me who lived a very similar story; possibly they are living it now.

By the end of this book, I pray you will make a life-changing decision to not allow the enemy of your soul to lie to you another day. After all, like a vapor—life is too short. Don't waste your life living a lie.

Jamie Massey

The Lie

CHAPTER ONE
THE LIE:

"You Can't Handle Your Circumstances..."

"The thief comes only to steal and kill and destroy; I have come that you may have life, and have it to the full."
John 10:10 KJV

"Oh God, do you see me, do you hear me?" The violence of the storm raging within me pounded viciously against every carefully constructed wall I had erected to keep me safe. Systematically, the walls of protection crumbled as I sank to my knees. I scrambled through my thoughts searching desperately for one sliver of light to keep the encroaching darkness from swallowing me whole.

Through the fog I heard a voice say, "Look at you; you're a mess. You're going crazy. By the time you're twenty years old, you'll be institutionalized." My mind began to race. Memories of my two great aunts, tortured and finally institutionalized by mental illness, taunted me relentlessly.

"You're just like them; you can't handle it." Maybe the voice was telling the truth.

By the age of fifteen, I was falling apart emotionally. I had no strength left to fight. My coping mechanisms had collapsed, leaving me frightened, vulnerable, and doubting my sanity.

Suddenly, awareness began to pierce through the darkness like tiny pinholes of light, vividly exposing my surroundings. I was lying on my face, my school books scattered around me in disarray. I had collapsed on the floor in the entry way of my home. The voice was right—I was a mess.

How did I get to this place of hopelessness? After all, I have a relationship with Jesus Christ. I am filled with His precious Holy Spirit. Doesn't that guarantee victory for me? How did I get here?

I was born and raised in Pensacola, Florida – a city known for its beautiful beaches and tourist attractions. My father was employed at a nearby Naval Air Base Station as an aircraft engineer, while my mother, typical of women raising families during the 1960's carried out the role of wife and homemaker until we were much older.

Our home on 72nd Avenue was a simple three bedroom, one bath, block house, painted in a tropical green color with a side carport. In the front yard stood a tall, strong magnolia tree that often served as an apparatus to entertain me and my three sisters. We climbed as high as that tree would let us and even used its cones for ammunition for our war games with our neighborhood playmates. I guess you could say that all of us Jeter girls had a little bit of tomboy in us.

The front of our home was outlined by several bushes that formed an "L" shape down the drive and "the woods", as we called them, stood adjacent to the side yard. We loved to play in those woods – building forts, spending endless hours at hide and seek, and whatever creative games we could come up with. My parents bought the house before I was born, so even now, I remember it fondly as "home" even though the life that unfolded there was not always what we want life to be.

My parents met in a bar when my mother was 17 and my father was 27. Although both of them had been raised in church, neither of them were serving God at that time. They were young and impetuous, living it up and enjoying the freedom of a cultural revolution on the rise.

My father was quite the dancer. As a popular instructor at Arthur Murray Dance Studio, he knew all the right moves. He was a charming and handsome man, often called "Mr. Hollywood" because of his perfect teeth and bright smile. He had served as a sergeant in the army during the Korean War. His charismatic personality and strong leadership qualities made him likable to both men and women. However, women especially loved him and my mother fell head over heels the moment she met him.

My father, James Jeter, had already led a colorful life by the time he met my mother, Mary Ann Henderson. His mother worked hard to make sure that James and his eight siblings had the benefit of being raised right—planting the children in a Pentecostal church near their home in Alabama and overseeing their spiritual upbringing to the best of her ability.

He rarely spoke of his father and when he did it was with disdain. My grandfather was a womanizer which eventually led to divorce. My father often spoke of an encounter with God at the age of sixteen, when he felt certain God called him into the ministry. He described that experience like a bolt of lightening that came out of heaven and hit him in the chest, knocking him flat on his back. This powerful encounter with God transformed him, and over the next year he spent countless hours in the woods near his home praying and seeking God for direction. He often recounted the glorious meetings with God when he left the woods feeling like he was on cloud nine.

However, when he joined the Army at the age of seventeen his relationship with God changed. He was exposed to a whole new world and that world affected him negatively. After leaving the Army, he attended Lee College in Cleveland, Tennessee. He was going to pursue God's call for his life but fell back into the old patterns of sin he practiced in the Army. After violating a rule he was asked to leave the Christian College and this often troubled him years later.

After leaving college, he met and married a woman and fathered a son named after him. Their marriage was rocky as my father became more and more abusive, so she left him, taking their son with her. I was seven years old when I found out I had a brother.

Mary Ann Henderson was the youngest of six children. Her mother was faithful to take her to the Baptist church regularly. Her father was an alcoholic who abused her mother. Mom would tell stories of witnessing the abuse as a child. One story that seemed to trouble her the most occurred when she was about five years old. She recalled seeing her father beat her mother so severely in the chest that her mother started vomiting blood.

Mother had an older sister that she loved dearly. Elaine, who suffered from the effects of her unstable home environment started drinking heavily at a young age. My grandmother worried about her troublesome behavior and would often send my mother, who was a young teenager at the time, to watch out for her older sister at the bars. Mom was more than accustomed to the role of caretaker. As a young girl she helped her father find his way to the local bar and patiently waited outside for him until he was stone-drunk and out of money.

Then she guided him safely home. For years, she took on the role of caring for her alcoholic father. Doing the same for her older sister, though she was only a teenager, seemed a natural way of life to her.

Mother was a beauty to behold. Looking much older than her seventeen years, many compared her looks to a cross between Elizabeth Taylor and Jennifer Jones. No wonder she caught the eye of James Jeter. One of those times when my mom was at the club "watching-out" for Elaine, she met my father.

A few dances, a few drinks, and my mother thought she was in love. It wasn't long into their relationship when mother discovered she was pregnant. Dad tried to convince her to have an abortion. After all, she was young and they really didn't know one another well. My mother had a different plan. She wanted to have this baby and she wanted to marry James Jeter. She was in love.

They married and concealed her pregnancy long enough for her to graduate from high school. In October, Shannon was born. Fourteen months later, Tonya was born. Nineteen months later, Demedra was born. These were extremely difficult years for my parents.

Money was tight and my father began having extramarital affairs. During this time they purchased the house on 72nd Avenue. Mother was determined they would be a family, even though their idea of what a "family" should be was still tainted by the environment they each were raised in. Caught up in the night life of partying and drinking, what began as an unstable union spiraled downward.

My father directed his explosive temper toward my mother, especially when he was drunk. He became increasingly abusive as the marriage progressed, feeling trapped in a double life that seemed to eat away at him. He loved his family—I have no doubt about that, but even so, he couldn't seem to break through the cycle of abuse and alcoholism that threatened to destroy the family he loved.

Looking back at that time, I wonder if my mother and father ever cried out to God in their helplessness to change. They were miserable and the fairytale marriage dissipated into a nightmare of financial distress, broken promises, and responsibilities they could not cope with.

Demedra was a beautiful baby with much promise. She wasn't even a year old when she got sick. Mother knew something was terribly wrong with her and her fears were confirmed when the doctor diagnosed her with Tuberculosis Meningitis of the spine.

The Doctors worked hard to save Demedra's life. She underwent treatments and surgeries but her condition only worsened. It was during one of her surgeries that the hospital chaplain paid mother a visit in the waiting room. He talked to her about Christ and His death.

The chaplain shared the salvation message with my mother by drawing a broken bridge with a huge gap. He used a hand-drawn illustration to show her how our sins separate us from God. He explained to her how there was no way that we could get to the Father because our sins had separated us from Him. He drew a cross through the gap to link the broken bridge and told her Christ has made it possible for us to have a personal relationship with our Heavenly Father. As Mother listened, God was working on her heart, drawing her closer to Him—bridging the gap.

After one of the surgeries, Demedra was rendered blind. There was no way she would ever regain her vision. Mother cried out to God in the hospital chapel and told the Lord that she didn't care if Demedra was blind. She said, "Lord, I just want her. It doesn't matter if she's blind. Please let her live." But God had a bigger plan in mind and used this tragic time to draw James and Mary Ann to Him, effecting generations to come.

Demedra was just thirteen months old when she died. Mother was so devastated she refused to go home until all the baby items were removed from the house. My older sisters remember the funeral. Tonya recalls thinking Demedra was asleep—she looked like a baby doll in her casket. The day of my sister's funeral, there was a beautiful poem in the local newspaper that my mother clipped and kept in a photo album along with a lock of Demedra's hair. The poem, written by Ben Burroughs, was entitled *Sketches*.

> *When someone you held very dear...is called by God to rest... the pain of weary loneliness...will be your greatest test... for when you lose a loved one... life loses all its charm... doubts and fears will fill your heart... with mountains of alarm... time will hang heavy over you... days and nights will be long...every tune you listen to... will be a plaintive song... it's then you'll fully realize... the comfort God can give... He is the only recourse... the spirit's sedative... through Him you'll gain the faith you need... and strength to follow through... He knows that those who walk alone... possess a sordid view... and so God gives the gift of prayer... to banish skies of gray... the someone you held very dear... is but a prayer away[1].*

After the funeral, mother struggled with her grief. One night while trying to sleep she saw a vision of a spirit drawing her. She said she knew it was Demedra trying to tell her she wanted her

---

1   Sketches; Author: Ben Burroughs; published by The Pensacola News, date, Copy Right unknown

to be where she was—with God. This caused my mother and father to seek answers. They decided to visit a Pentecostal church on a Sunday morning; it was a decision that changed their lives.

Mother said she couldn't recall what the minister's sermon was about, but all she wanted was to get to the altar as soon as possible. When the pastor gave the invitation for salvation my mother jumped up and shouted, "I'm tired of living for the devil. I want to live for Jesus!" She ran to the altar and my father joined her and together they were gloriously set free and forgiven by the power of God's love through Jesus Christ.

James and Mary Ann experienced a radical change that morning. They became devoted followers of the Lord Jesus Christ. They were active in their local church serving in many different capacities, but each still felt a void from the loss of Demedra that would not go away.

Mother often said, there is no pain worse than the loss of a child. She thought if she could have another baby that perhaps the depth of her loss would be replaced with joy. But there was a problem; she couldn't conceive. Her doctor informed her she would probably never have another child. She refused to accept the doctor's prognosis and immediately asked the women of the church to pray for a miracle. She wanted another baby. The women of the church began to pray. If you need a miracle I am convinced if you get a group of determined, word-filled women together you're going to hear from God.

It wasn't long before it was confirmed my mother was pregnant. Miraculously, nine months later, Jamie Ann Jeter (named after both parents) was born. My father was so thrilled to have been given another child that he did something he didn't know to do with his other daughters. He decided to give me back to God. After Mom and Dad brought me home from the hospital he went into the room where my crib was and shut the door. He picked me up, knelt down on the floor and raised me up toward heaven.

Crying, he prayed and thanked God for another child. Right then and there my father dedicated my life to the Lord. He was so afraid of losing another child that he couldn't wait for a church service to offer me to God. He wanted all of his daughters given to God for His use. My parents were doubly blessed when they found out mother was pregnant again and thirteen months after I was born, along came my sister, Myla. God blessed my parents with two more daughters after the loss of their precious Demedra.

It appeared their lives were moving in a positive direction; *some might even call it—perfect.*

CHAPTER TWO
THE LIE:

"Your Home is Perfect..."

"Jesus knew their thoughts and said to them, 'Every kingdom divided against itself will be ruined, and every city or household divided against itself will not stand.'"
Matthew 12:25 NIV

I lived in what I considered to be the perfect home, up to the age of nine. We were the kind of family that went to church every time the church doors were open. We had family devotion each night that included turning the television off.

My father gathered all of us together in the living room for time with God. James Jeter may not have stood behind a pulpit to preach the gospel, but we heard many of his sermons during family devotion time. After my father shared the Word of God with us, we would all find a place to kneel and pray. I loved to kneel next to my mother and listen to her prayers. My father would pray in his loud, articulate voice with much authority, but my mother would pray quietly, and yet I knew her words were powerful.

My parents were both involved in church activities. My mother was a strong alto and sang in the choir as well as special musical groups. She was a prayer warrior and attended the women's prayer meetings regularly. During the altar ministry time you would find Mary Ann kneeling and praying with intensity for the women who had responded to the altar call. She lingered in the altars as long as people were praying there. I can still recall the beauty of my mother in the presence of the Lord.

It was not unusual to find the Jeter children asleep on the church bench on Sunday evenings. There were times when my mother awakened us well after midnight to walk to the car, after she finished praying with everyone. Her relationship with the Lord was unique. God had so gloriously saved her and in Him she found the answers she had desperately searched for.

When I was a small child, I remember hearing my mother singing *Amazing Grace* in the kitchen while she cooked one evening. Although I was very young, I knew something powerful was happening. I stood at the entry way of the kitchen and watched as my mother sang standing at the stove. Her eyes were closed and tears were rolling down her cheeks. Suddenly she was so enraptured by God's presence she fell on the floor, slain under the power of the Holy Spirit. No one had touched her. No one had prayed for her; yet the power of God was so strong in that room she could not stand any longer.

As she lay on the floor trembling under the power of God's Spirit, I walked over to her and stood gazing down, sensing something supernatural. I was so young, four or five years old, but I knew God was speaking to my mother. I'd seen my mom like this at church on several occasions, but I had never seen her like this at home. My father came and picked me up and took me to the living room where we all sat and waited on Mom to return to the *natural realm*. This made such an impression on me and a deep desire for the things of God began to stir within me. From my earliest memories I have hungered and yearned for Him, but there was something about what I sensed that day that set my course for life.

I was approximately six years old when I accepted the Lord as my personal Savior at Sunday school one bright, warm Florida morning. Every week in Sunday school my teacher had us fold our hands and bow our heads at the end of class. She led us in a song called *Into My Heart*[2]as a benediction. The song said,

"Into my heart. Into my heart. Come in to my heart, Lord Jesus.
Come in to stay. Come in today. Come in to my heart, Lord Jesus."

---

2   Into My Heart by Harry D. Clarke © 1924, Ren. 1952 Hope Publishing Company, Carol Stream, IL 60188. All rights reserved. Used by permission.

A very simple song but it said everything I needed to say. Although we sang the song every week, something happened to me that day. Tears welled up and brimmed over, flowing freely down my cheeks. As I sang the words with my lips I said in my heart, "Lord, I mean it today. I really want you to come in to my heart today." That moment I received Jesus as my personal Savior and my sins, however many they were at such a young age, were washed away. I may have been young, but I realized I was born a sinner in need of redemption.

My sisters and I became active in our home church. My older sisters were examples to me and Myla through their dedication to serve in various leadership roles. Shannon and Tonya were talented singers and musicians who sang in special groups in the church. As Myla and I grew older, we all sang together as The Jeter Sisters Quartet. My parents were exceptionally proud of our talents. On many occasions, we girls entertained ourselves by breaking into song as we journeyed somewhere in the car or sat around the house. Often mother joined in and I remember my dad grinning from ear to ear. Sometimes he requested a special song such as, *Ten Thousand Years*[3], recorded

---

3   Song Title: Ten Thousand Years; author: Elmer Cole, copyright 1970. Bridge Building Music, Inc (BMI) a division of Brentwood-Benson Music Publishing, Inc Used by permission.

by Dottie Rambo. It was one of his favorites. Dad would sit and cry as we sang:

> *"Ten thousand years... We'll just be started.*
> *Ten thousand years...We've just begun.*
> *The battle is over and the victory is won!*
> *Ten thousand years... We've just begun."*

Music seemed to bind our hearts together in a special way that's hard to explain even today. We could sense God's presence in our worship. A rich heritage was developing and the roots of that heritage were growing deep within my heart. I longed to have the close fellowship with God that my mother seemed to have, and the deep knowledge of God my father possessed.

My dad taught an adult Bible class each Sunday morning. His class overflowed with people wanting to sit under his anointed teaching. My father was a history buff and loved to study different time periods, such as the Civil War and great generals of the past, but he especially loved to study Bible history. He loved to challenge me and my sisters to memorize complete chapters of the Bible.

I was always—my whole life—an early riser, as was my father. There were many mornings I awoke to find him up and studying his Bible. Sunday mornings he made it a point to rise extra early to spend time with the Lord in preparation for his class.

Because my father had a special anointing to deliver God's Word, people anticipated his ministry time. My father eventually served as the Sunday School Superintendent at our church, coordinating the adult Christian Education Department.

James Jeter was a gifted story teller. His dramatic and demonstrative antics captivated his audience and his commanding voice demanded attention. As children we sat on the edge of our seats, watching and listening to colorful stories about his childhood.

Being raised "dirt poor" in Alabama, as he used to say, gave my father a lot of juicy material for story time. At times he told us about his experience in Korea, but the war stories seemed to trouble him. His encounter with Christ at sixteen years old was his favorite story. Oh, how he would light up each time he shared that experience. Sadly, there were also memories that seemed to torment him relentlessly. He got so caught up in the failures of yesterday he became lost in pain. When the accuser of the brethren, satan, threw those memories up to him he grew distant, worried, and quiet. Since by nature he was a boisterous, lively man, when he was in that deep place of anguish we all tended to avoid him. My mother knew to be cautious around him during those times, fearing she might trigger an explosive outburst.

Although my father renewed his relationship with Christ he still struggled with his flesh. Anger and violence were still very real issues in his life, hidden to those who knew him as the anointed teacher and church leader. My mother was, more often than not, the object of his frustration. She feared that the peaceful Christian façade would one day shatter, sending our home back into the tumultuous throws of abuse and addiction.

I only have two memories of his explosive temper during those early years. Once was when I was about two or three years old, I remember my father hitting my mother and feeling afraid. Then suddenly Daddy was giving everybody ice cream. My next memory has stayed with me in detail because it altered everything I thought and believed until then.

That warm Sunday morning me and my sisters were getting ready for church as usual. My mother was standing at the ironing board tending to all of our dresses. My father was pacing back and forth in frustration because we were running late. This should have been no surprise to Dad. We were late *every* Sunday. My mother was chronically late everywhere she went. By now she was employed as a Teacher's Aide but she risked her job each day with her tardy lifestyle. My father, on the other hand, was extremely punctual. As an aircraft engineer with the Naval Air Station base, he was rigidly programmed to be on time—if not early. This had always been a source of contention between them, but that morning something deeper seemed to be gnawing at him; it wasn't just the tardiness that set him off.

I lay on the floor in the living room watching our regular Christian music program we routinely watched on Sunday mornings as we got ready for church. I heard my parents arguing, as usual, and thought nothing of it. Suddenly their arguing grew more intense and I saw my father pull his fist back to hit my mother as my mother raised the iron up to protect herself. Tonya jumped in between them trying to prevent the violence from erupting. In the scuffle she was accidentally burned. Tonya's injury caused my parents to settle down and begin talking.

Although I was relieved the fighting stopped, I didn't like the way the conversation was going. The atmosphere was cold, as if a spirit of death entered and hovered over our family. My older sisters were crying and I felt confused and afraid. I was naïve, sheltered, and completely clueless. What did it mean? Why was everyone crying? What was happening to our perfect home? That's when I heard the word that was about to turn my perfect world upside down—*divorce*.

I was unaware of it, but apparently trouble had been brewing between my parents for quite a while. It seemed to intensify when my half brother, David, came to stay with us one summer. I was seven years old and he was seventeen.

Mom and Dad tried to explain why this new brother suddenly appeared in our lives, but the whole situation was confusing to me. I was excited to meet him, but couldn't figure out how this was possible. After all, we were the perfect Christian family. How did this fit into our world?

David was a rowdy, angry child, who resented my father. I remember the first time I saw him. He had long hair, proudly worn in two braids. He had dark, American Indian features like his mother and a smile that could take your breath away like my father. He was a handsome young man, but he'd already made some very bad choices with his life. Mother didn't accept Dad's first wife coming back into the picture and division quickly hit our home. It began to feel like a combat zone. Their arguing became more frequent and intense. Also during that period I noticed our family devotion time fading. Something was going terribly wrong but I was too young to understand it.

It seemed that the very thing my mother feared most crept into our home unexpectedly. That's how subtle the enemy is. With my father rehearsing his past failures, even in light of his knowledge and wisdom of the Word, a hairline crack opened and that was all the enemy needed to lodge a wedge into my parent's marriage.

Unfortunately, the wedge was deep and it created more than momentary disharmony in our home. It would rapidly dissolve everything my parents believed, leaving us vulnerable to the hideous assault that loomed on the horizon. *The "perfect home" was about to crumble as we bought into the lie... divorce is unforgivable.*

CHAPTER THREE
THE LIE:

"Divorce is Unforgivable"

"'I hate divorce,' says the Lord God of Israel..."
Malachi 2:16 KJV

Does a nine year old understand the extremes that life can dish out? Looking back at that year of my life it seems the glorious, miraculous presence of the Lord and the stifling evil presence of satan both took center stage as a battle raged within the only sanctuary I knew—my home.

Our church held a week of revival that was so powerful the pastor decided to continue into the next week. We were in church every night, but something strange and wonderful was happening in me as we turned the corner into the second week.

The evangelist presented a compelling invitation to come pray at the altar. I was sitting next to a friend who was a few years older than me. She decided to respond to the invitation so I followed her cue and we made our way to the place of prayer.

In my home church, the men met for prayer on one side of the altar and the women on the other. My friend and I knelt in the women's area and several older women gathered around to pray with us. Most of them gathered around my friend, sensing perhaps that she was old enough to understand the call of the Lord. At this point I was more of an observer. However the more they talked with my friend about receiving from God a deeper experience they called the baptism of the Holy Spirit, the more curious I became. As I observed and listened to the women leading my friend into this glorious, encounter with God, I began to cry, desiring this same experience.

Everything they told my friend to do, I did as well. They said to my friend, "Sweetie, lift your hands." So, I lifted my hands just like my friend. They said to her, "Say, Praise the Lord!" So, I uttered softly "Praise the Lord!"

A precious woman saw my tears and knelt next to me asking, "Would you like to receive the baptism of the Holy Spirit too?" I nodded with tears sprinkling my cheeks. This sweet godly woman began leading me to receive a spiritual transformation that truly altered the course of my life.

She instructed me to lift my hands and praise the Lord aloud. I was already doing that, but I instinctively responded to her instruction by fervently expressing praises to God. Little did I know what was about to occur—little did I know that a supernatural encounter with God that night would forever change me.

Suddenly, I was caught up in the spiritual realm. I temporarily lost all concept of what was happening around me. I don't know if it was a vision or if I completely left my body. I would never try to compare with the great Apostle Paul, but from this experience I understand what he meant when he said in 2 Corinthians 12:2 (NKJ), "I know a man in Christ who fourteen years ago—whether in the body I do not know, or whether out of the body I do not know, God knows—such a one was caught up to the third heaven."

It is difficult to explain what happened to me, but I was truly "caught up" in another realm. I saw myself standing before a great cloud or mist. This cloud moved as though it were alive and the voice of God spoke audibly from within the cloud. It was not with an earthly language, but as God spoke, my spirit understood. As soon as I heard His words my spirit-man comprehended. I spoke back, but also with my spirit. It was as if whatever I thought, He heard and whatever He thought, I heard. It was glorious. How a child could experience and know such a thing, I can't explain.

The Lord shared His love with me and I understood; He would never stop loving me.

For God so loved the world, that he gave his only begotten Son, that whosoever believeth in

uld *not perish, but have everlasting life.*
(John 3.16)

We cannot fathom the depth of God's love for us. He "SO" loves us that He "GAVE" us His very best; His Son, Jesus Christ. I realized, as I stood there in His presence, that He can't help but love us. It is His nature and His desire to love. Oh friend, don't let anything you've done or anywhere life has taken you cause you to doubt His very personal love for you. God cannot love us any less or any more than He does right at this moment. I believe the key to total surrender in Him is unlocked when we finally accept the unconditional love that He expresses to us, through Christ. A fully surrendered life is a blessed, abundant life filled with love.

God also shared a gift with me—joy! Up until that moment, I never experienced true joy to that degree. As I stood before Him, unspeakable joy swept over me. I began laughing in his presence. The beautiful thing about this part of the experience is that God laughed with me. It was as if God took pleasure in my laughter. My joy made Him smile. You may think it is irreverent to laugh in the presence of God, but I was only nine and didn't know any grown-up concepts like reverence. I was so overwhelmed with joy that it made me laugh. The Father was so pleased with my joy, He joined in. Yes, God and I laughed together. I believe God laughs and rejoices with us. Listen to what the scripture says in Zephaniah 3:17.

"The LORD thy God in the midst of thee [is] mighty; he will save, he will rejoice over thee with joy; he will rest in his love, he will joy over thee with singing".

Again the scripture is clear concerning the importance of joy in our lives. Listen to the words of Nehemiah 8:10:

"...For the joy of the LORD is your strength."

With the rise of depression and anxiety among God's people, I think a good dose of joy is healing. Know that the Heavenly Father laughs with you and is blessed by your joy. He longs to laugh and rejoice with His children.

God then shared another gift with me—life. This life wasn't just IN me, it was ON me. It was as if *life* was dancing all about me. It was electric and divine. The *life* of God is powerful.

Jesus said unto her, I am the resurrection, and the life: he that believeth in me, though he were dead, yet shall he live. (John 11:25)

This gift of life can resurrect anything: dead dreams, goals, visions, relationships, disasters, circumstances; no situation is ever final when the author of all *life* shows up. As I stood before the Lord receiving this revelation of life I was filled with faith and confidence in the life-giver.

Jesus saith unto him, I am the way, the truth, and the life: no man cometh unto the Father, but by me. (John 14:6)

Friend, trust the life-giver today. He will restore every lifeless place in you if you will but believe.

One final thing occurred in His presence that I find difficult to verbalize. I felt like God placed a warm blanket over me. I was completely submerged in a feeling of safety. I felt securely embraced by the strong arm of the Lord. I realized I would never be alone. No matter what happened, I knew with confidence that God would never leave me.

"...for he hath said, I will never leave thee, nor forsake thee." (Hebrews 13:5)

When I left the spiritual realm and became alert once again to my surroundings, I was flat on my back and completely disoriented. I didn't know how I had gotten to the place where I was lying, and I didn't know how long I had been there. When you are in the spirit realm you lose all concept of time in the natural realm. As I started to get up, I heard words coming out of my mouth in a language I had never been taught. I received the baptism of the Holy Spirit and my prayer language was evident. The dear woman who had been praying with me called for my mother.

"Mary Ann, come listen to Jamie!" My mother came to my side immediately, rejoicing with me as I continued weeping and speaking in my prayer language.

I didn't fully understand what occurred that night when I was nine, but I knew it was a divine encounter. I kept it mostly to myself until I was grown. I don't believe that God gives us supernatural experiences because we earn it, deserve it, or are loved by the Father more than others, or because He sees us as more special in any way.

We are all special to the Father and He is no respecter of persons. If God chooses to visit us in a divine, supernatural way it is because He knows what is ahead of us and we will need that experience to make it through. I didn't understand at the time why God chose to visit me in such as way, but I soon learned. The bond that formed in my heart with the Father that night kept me intact emotionally through the pain and uncertainty that was yet to come.

Just weeks following this encounter with God, my parents called us to the living room to announce their decision to divorce. It was Shannon's 16th birthday. I remember tugging on one of my older sisters and asking, "What is divorce?". What happened in the living room that day didn't make sense. My perfect world was rapidly deteriorating.

The divorce altered everything we knew to be true about our family and our faith. My parents made a fate-changing decision that day not to go back to church. No matter what happened to them however, they mutually agreed that we girls must continue going to church without them. My oldest sister, Shannon, bore the load of responsibility for us girls. As the oldest child, their decision was hard on her. My sister Tonya began questioning and testing her faith. Her battle to understand how my parents could just walk away from their faith brought about much of her struggle. My younger sister, Myla, and myself were so confused that we internalized much of our emotions. We simply were not equipped to deal with the instability, anger and upheaval of divorce.

You see, to my parents divorce was the unpardonable sin. The enemy subtly used the scripture against them. Passages like "I hate divorce," says the Lord God of Israel," (Malachi 2:16) took on the pointing finger of a vengeful God in their minds, separating them from the body of Christ and the personal relationship with the only One that could heal and restore.

The enemy will always twist God's words to suit his purpose. My parents bought into a lie, as have many of God's people; God would never forgive them for making the decision to divorce. They felt God could never do anything with their lives and therefore, fueled by guilt, they hid from their maker. Like Adam and Eve sewing fig leaves to hide their shame, my parents sewed the fig leaves of shame about themselves and ran from God with all their might.

Living with shame and guilt is a deeply tormenting way of life and you can never truly escape it without the power of God, no matter how hard you try. My parents so skillfully sewed the fig leaves of shame and guilt over their lives and continued sewing until this garment adorned our entire family. Suddenly, I too began wearing this garment and for some reason I believed the lie that—*it was all my fault.*

CHAPTER FOUR
THE LIE:

"It's All Your Fault"

"My guilt has overwhelmed me like a burden too heavy to bear."
Psalm 38:4 KJV

As a child reared in a dysfunctional family, I often felt guilt and didn't understand why. The chaos of our home dictated the unspoken finger-pointing of blame. "After all, someone is responsible for all the pain and it must be me," I reasoned. So, we each in our own way, tried to escape the guilty feelings. I dove into school work to avoid the negative aftermath of guilt. I tried hard to make my parents proud. I desperately wanted to see them happy so I worked hard to excel; thus the illusion of escaping guilt. No matter how hard I tried, I couldn't unburden myself.

In Job 9:20 the scripture says, *"Even if I were innocent, my mouth would condemn me; if I were blameless, it would pronounce me guilty"*.

Job spoke from the depths of a very difficult trial. He had lost his family, his possessions, and his health. However, in this passage he reveals the battle that all of mankind faces; self-condemnation. Even when reason dictates we are innocent, our mind still struggles to overcome guilt. Unfortunately, we can go through life blaming ourselves and bearing the weight of fault, even if it makes no sense to do so. Even though I was young, I latched on to one personal promise from God in Romans 8:1-2:

There is therefore now no condemnation to them which are in Christ Jesus, who walk not after the flesh, but after the Spirit. For the law of the Spirit of life in Christ Jesus hath made me free from the law of sin and death.

I escaped into my studies when the tension at home was overbearing. Reading Florida's history allowed me to fantasize of a more simplistic time. Working a math problem and solving it made me feel like problems did have solutions if you work hard enough to discover them. My teacher took notice of my aptitude. She told my mother she thought I was a gifted student and needed a greater challenge in my school work. She recommended testing me to find out how I might do in an accelerated learning environment.

My mother was so proud. I remember the talk we had about this wonderful chance to move to another class—the class for "the smart people." Out of nowhere, I began to panic. What if I fail her? What if I disappoint her? Self doubt was doing it's best work; leading me directly down the path toward self-condemnation. The night before the testing was horrible. I couldn't sleep and my stomach ached all night. I was so nervous that I couldn't concentrate or keep any thing in my stomach. My mother knew the anxiety I was feeling had a grip on me; mind, body, and soul. She did her best to calm and comfort me, and while her encouragement helped some, it was not enough to relieve the panic.

I can't remember very much about the actual test except the final outcome. I didn't score high enough to be accepted to the class for gifted students. I overheard my mother making excuses for me as she explained my nervous behavior to the teacher. I was overwhelmingly disappointed and ashamed of myself as we left school that day. In my mind, I let my parents down. They so badly needed a thread of joy in their life and I had stolen their opportunity to experience it when I failed the test. It was my fault. I'm not sure why I felt responsible for restoring my parents joy, but for some reason I accepted this as my assignment and having failed, I berated myself for doing such a poor job.

For the next ten months my parents navigated the emotional rollercoaster of divorce; a decision that created a dramatic impact in our lifestyle. During that period my sisters and I continued to attend church; the one place that seemed to ease my troubled soul and give me a sense of stability. Our church family stood with us through the turmoil, never ceasing to pray for us.

One of the hardest changes for me to accept came when my parents started dating other people. It was painfully uncomfortable for me. My father moved out of the house to a place of his own and I missed him greatly. My heart ached terribly for him. I remember feeling we must have done something horribly wrong for Dad to leave. My precious mother was clawing her way through the emotional confusion and losing the battle—that much was obvious. I remember watching her get dressed up to go out on a date and sensing her awkwardness. I told her how beautiful she looked, but inside, I felt sorry for her. Was she at peace with the single life?

During the season of divorce Dad picked me and Myla up to spend the night at his place. I still recall my excitement about spending time with him and finally seeing where and how he was living without us. A friend offered to let my father stay in his house and it was a beautiful home, but Dad was both distant and contemplative. Trying to figure my father out was always a challenge and a mystery. He seemed so out of place in his new environment and yet, unlike my mother, he was at peace.

A beautiful placid lake stretched in back of the house. Not only was the setting picturesque, but the home boasted a private pier. Dad planned our time together as a fishing adventure because that was one of his favorite hobbies. It provided a needed outlet for him to relax and think. At one time, he owned his own fishing boat and made good use of it until he had to sell it for financial reasons. Oh how special I felt that day, to be fishing with my dad. Spending a lazy afternoon on the pier turned out to be therapeutic for all of us.

Dad tried to discuss the divorce. He seemed truly interested in how we were dealing with the aftermath. As he talked, he appeared relieved. The divorce provided a refuge from the secret stress that accompanies a less than monogamous married life. He tried to explain that my parent's decision to divorce wouldn't change how much he loved us. He was more than apologetic over all that was happening between him and mom and the impact it was having on us. It was obvious that he too was trying to process an enormous load of guilt and shame, but at the same time, he appeared determined to move on.

Watching my parents begin to date was strange to me. The club scene my parents knew so well was once again a familiar pattern; church had vanished completely from their lifestyle. Divorce did nothing to quell the anger and bitterness between them; if anything, it escalated. The fighting continued even after the divorce; mostly fueled by jealousy as they dated other people.

One traumatic episode particularly stands out in my mind when I think back on that confusing period in my childhood. It was late afternoon and we were driving home. We passed my father's truck going the opposite direction. Angrily, my mother slammed on the brakes and turned the car around in hot pursuit.

"What's going on," I yelled at my mother, trying to fight back the panic. I'm not sure what frightened me more—her outburst of uncontrolled rage or her erratic driving. Mom was furious about seeing a woman in the truck with Dad. She caught up with him and began honking the horn and flashing her lights; screaming out the window for him to pull over.

Her reckless driving endangered everyone on the road. Dad finally pulled over. Mom jumped out of the car and Dad jumped out of the truck with a grin on his face like a prize fighter gloating after a big win. They began shouting at each other right in the middle of the parking lot of a gas station. As I looked out the car window into the cab of the truck, I saw the frightened expression on the face of my father's companion. I remember thinking she looked so young—no more than Shannon's age.

My mom just couldn't let go. I realized that day how much she still loved my dad and still wanted him. Were we standing in the way of our parent's happiness? I questioned everything. Maybe if we weren't around they might work things out. This seemed all the more of an accurate assessment of our situation when mom sent Myla and me to live with her sister in North Carolina that summer. She and dad decided to work on their relationship and they must have decided that it would help to have time alone.

The road rage incident was but one of the many rollercoaster rides that accompanied my parents time of separation and divorce. The proverbial quote "can't live with him, can't live without him" certainly applied to my mother's feelings toward my father. Although my father loved my mother, I think it was difficult for him to feel truly happy in a monogamous relationship.

Their decision to work on their relationship was not merely driven by love on my father's part. Perhaps more by the desire to be someone he wasn't is a more apt description. I think he wanted to be a good father, a good husband, and a good provider—but the dark side of his personality always seemed to win out eventually. Nevertheless, my mother and my father were as miserable apart as they were together, so off we went for a summer adventure while they sorted through the debris of their marriage.

My Aunt Joy graciously took care of us. They lived in a beautiful, large home on the top of a mountain. The view was spectacular. Unlike our humble home in Florida, with its flat terrain, my aunt's property offered wide open space and abundant opportunities for my imagination to soar. I enjoyed playing with my seven cousins and my Aunt Joy was a wonderful mother. The fun we had that summer will always stay with me.

Even though I was having the time of my life, I still experienced periods of intense homesickness. I cried so hard and my aunt did her best to console me, but the emotions were overwhelming. I felt like I would never see my parents again. Thankfully, the separation from my parents was short lived. By the end of the summer, Mom and Dad reconciled and decided to remarry. God really heard my secret prayers.

My parents were reconciling! I was filled with joy and excitement as I imagined our home returning to its "perfect" status. It was 1976, the year of our country's Bicentennial celebration; the 200th birthday of the signing of the Declaration of Independence. People everywhere were declaring liberty and freedom, and I felt the revelry in my spirit as I regained hope for our freedom from guilt and the stigma of divorce. Surely my parents' remarriage would resolve the chaos that ruled our lives.

My excitement soon turned to elation when I realized that I would be attending my own parents wedding. How cool was that? And what a beautiful wedding it was. Mom was dressed in a floral gown of powder blue and Dad was handsome as ever in his matching tuxedo. My mother wanted to make sure it was a "real" wedding unlike the first time when they stood before a judge. This time she went all out, excitedly planning the ceremony and deliberating over the décor. She planned a fabulous reception with the cutting of a traditional wedding cake as the highlight of the festivities. A professional photographer tagged around with us to capture the bliss of my parent's wedding day.

Friends and family joyously witnessed the recommitment of love and promise of a brand new future. I remember the occasion so vividly, listening to my parents recite their vows before us, their children, and God their maker. To me, it was official, unlike the first time they married. This was a church wedding with our pastor praying God's blessings over the solemn vows. This time it had to work, I reasoned. My confused, torn heart was on the mend.

I made some vows of my own that day. I was determined to behave in such a way that the joy my parents felt would never end because of something I did. No way was I going to get in the way of their happiness. I was going to make sure I worked extra hard to make things as easy as possible. I would make them proud and give them no reason for disappointment. Yes, I would be the perfect church girl who prayed hard and did everything possible to help keep this family together. *I was going to fix it.*

CHAPTER FIVE
THE LIE:

"You Have to Fix It"

*"Two are better than one, because they have a good return for
their work: If one falls down, his friend can help him up.
But pity the man who falls and has no one to help him up!"
Ecclesiastes 4:9-10 NIV*

After my parent's remarriage, our home returned to a state of normalcy from outward appearances. The peace was short-lived, however. Before long, the fighting between them started again. This time, Mom and Dad became consumed with the partying scene, and along with it, came the binge drinking and drug use.

The weekends were a blur of drunkenness, predawn fights, and late morning hangovers. The emotional rollercoaster ride was filled with jealous accusations between my parents, rooted in their infidelity. It was a game of who would provoke the other first into their jealous rages. Details of their affairs were sent hurling around like bullets during their drunken fights. My sisters and I witnessed and heard things children should never have to witness, nor hear about their parents.

In dysfunctional families the parents become the children and the children the parents. Our family was a classic model and we could have been the poster children for the Dysfunctional Homes of America Association, had there been such a thing.

It was during these unsettling years I began to view my sister Shannon as the protector of the family; my surrogate mother. She made sure we had transportation and food even if it meant stepping up to receive the wrath of my mom and dad.

Late one evening I was awakened by my sister, Tonya, and a family friend who told me and Myla to put on our robes quickly. I could hear fighting in the living room. It wasn't the usual voices of Mother and Dad, but it was familiar. Trying to shake off the sleep and make sense of what was transpiring I asked, "What's the matter? Where are we going?"

"Hurry," I was told and we were whisked into the living room. There, looming in a drunken state was my dad and standing guard, protectively, was my sister Shannon.

Dad was threatening her, "You tell me right now where your mother is."

"I don't know," Shannon replied as she slowly made her way behind a chair. Dad was getting closer and more angry as he moved in toward her.

"Yes, you do know where she is. Tell me," and he dashed around the chair to grab her. She quickly made her way into the dining room, barely making her escape. As she lured him away from the door, we hurried out to the waiting car. In a flash, Shannon managed to escape and jump into the car with us and we sped away to a place of safety.

Where we went is unclear. Occasionally our church family provided a haven to us as we waited for the turmoil to subside. Sometimes we just passed the time riding around until we knew the coast was clear. It all runs together in a muddy mess when I reflect on each episode. One thing is very clear—the trauma was relentless.

Ah, Shannon, our rescuer. How I looked up to her and depended on her steady hand for our security. Although, Dad was the more aggressive, violent, and hot-tempered one when high or drunk, Mother had her moments as well. It was one such occasion, when Shannon was pleading with Mother not to leave us to go party with Dad, that the defining line of security was set for me. Dad was determined to go out and Mother wouldn't allow him to leave without her. After all, he might meet someone at the bar and she couldn't let that happen.

I listened as Shannon argued with mother in the dining room.

"At least leave us money so we can get some food and a car so I can drive us where we need to go," Shannon begged.

"Of course, here are the keys" mother replied, the annoyance evident in the tone of her voice.

Suddenly, the built up anger of neglect and the responsibility no teenager should have to carry, came piercing through as Shannon became incensed with mother's selfish answers.

Shannon said something that sent mother spinning into a rage. I watched as mother pulled Shannon by the hair down to the ground, jumping on top of her, slapping her in the face and screaming profanities. Shannon tried to shield her face with her hands and arms as mother pulled her hair and continued hitting her. Dad quickly intervened, pulling Mother off of Shannon as she continued to scream and kick at my sister.

"You will never speak to me that way again," Mother demanded. I saw the hurt in Shannon's eyes and the anger that fostered her outburst. Yes, Shannon did what she had to do in order to take care of us. She was our rescuer.

In May of 1978, Shannon married her long-time boyfriend and first love, Jerry Bell. It was a beautiful wedding, filled with hope and promise. Jerry was a minister and soon after their marriage they took the position of youth pastors for our church. Since Shannon was no longer living in our home, I began to look to Tonya to fill the void of supervision and care. She dutifully stepped into the role and made sure we had transportation, food, and of course the covering of protection. Tonya did her share of breaking up drunken fights and stepping in to shield Mother from my father's abusive hand. I noticed God dealing with Tonya that summer. He was preparing her for a bright future which began to unfold the fall of 1978.

I remember in detail the day Tonya went to college. Dad, Mom, Tonya, Myla, and me piled into the car along with Tonya's belongings and drove from Pensacola to Cleveland, Tennessee where she would start school at Lee College. That weekend we walked the campus and helped Tonya settle into her new home in one of the girl's dorms. Dad shared stories of his college experience on that same campus. It was an exciting time and I could see the pride in Daddy's face knowing Tonya would be a student there. Dad often said to all of us through those growing up years he wanted us to attend Lee College. Shannon spent a semester there before her marriage to Jerry and now Tonya picked up the baton to carry on the tarnished, unfulfilled dream of my father.

I was twelve years old the day we drove away from the campus, waving good-bye to my sister. It was that moment that the weight of responsibility shifted to my shoulders. Now it was up to me to step into the role of caretaker; I would need to make sure Myla and I were protected; I would have to make a way for our basic needs to be met. It felt as if the load of the world came upon me that very moment as we drove toward home.

I sat directly behind the driver's side of the car, my face pressed against the window. Tears tumbled down my face. The atmosphere seemed oppressive and lonely. Dad and Mom were making conversation in the front seat and Myla was sitting beside me in the back. What was she thinking? Did she feel it too? Did she sense the fear? I cried out silently to God all the way home.

"Help me, Lord. I'm scared." My hushed cries seemed to echo through my entire body until it felt as though, surely, I would break into a million little pieces. Surely, God would answer. Surely, He knew my fear. In the midst of that suffocating darkness, He was the only hope I could reach for.

It seemed like an endless trip back to Pensacola and with each mile the weight became more oppressive. I didn't know exactly what was about to transpire for me and Myla, but Tonya had left me with a precious gift; the knowledge of prayer. And prayer became the security blanket that covered me through those dismal years of loneliness and fear.

I tried to encourage myself by dwelling on the thought that I would have a better life in the future, just like my sisters. That helped me ignore the chaos of the present, but blocking out the constant turmoil was practically impossible. How could you ignore the abuse my father was inflicting upon my mother, especially when it was increasingly more severe.

There was the time Dad pushed Mother out of a moving truck, dislocating her shoulder. There was the time he beat her so severely it burst her eardrum. There were the countless black eyes, and even one occasion, a beating that almost cost her the loss of her eyesight in one eye. My father was becoming more violent and my mother more driven to alcohol. Before the age of thirteen I was fully engaged in the role of "caretaker".

I would dart out of bed in the wee morning hours awakened by my mother's screams. I did what I had learned so well from my older sisters—protect my mother, my sister, and myself. I plunged into the chaos, screaming at my dad, begging him to stop hitting her, and if that didn't work, stepping in between them usually did. Sometimes the blows from my father accidentally fell on me, but at least it usually worked to stop the violence toward my mother.

The hangovers, as well as coming down from whatever high they were on, always troubled me because of the way they ravaged Mother's body. After one of their long binging weekends, mother must have taken something along with the alcohol that caused one of the worst incidents of all. She was in the bathroom vomiting severely and couldn't stop. Dad was pacing the floor in his robe, with fear etched on his face, that said he had not witnessed anything like this before.

I sat outside the bathroom door on the floor with my back against the wall crying and praying. "Please God, help Mom breathe," I begged, through my tears. The vomiting grew more severe.

"I may have to call 911 and get your mom some help," Dad said, but he didn't move toward the phone. I continued to pray and Dad continued to pace. "Breathe, Mary Ann," he told her over and over as though she could will herself to follow the command. She was nearly unconscious from the violence wracking her body. I knew she couldn't hear him.

"Daddy, please call for help. She's going to die if you don't," I cried. He seemed angry at the thought of calling someone but I was willing to risk his anger if it would save my mother's life.

Maybe whatever substance caused her aggressive sickness would bring too much trouble, I reasoned. That's why he's waiting to call for help. Other than my cries, I sat frozen, paralyzed by the fear that Mom may not survive this time. I prayed with everything in me, begging God to please hear me. Eventually she started to breathe and collapsed on the floor.

"Thank God," I moaned. Dad helped Mother off of the bathroom floor and onto the bed. I saw the pain in his eyes and the apologies that often followed his guilty conscience began to spill out of his mouth. He even tenderly stroked mother and wept. He meant it.

I was twelve years old when the parenting role became mine. I was determined to do my best in my newfound responsibility and to do it well. Along with Shannon and Jerry, I leaned heavily on our young pastor and his wife for emotional support. They often picked me and my sister, Myla, up for church since they lived rather close to our home. They knew the hostile environment we endured and did their best to help any way they could.

I learned much from them, but one of the most valuable things I learned was what a healthy, functioning, family looked like. They had three young daughters and I often babysat for them, allowing me to witness firsthand the way they treated one another. Oh, how I longed for a family like theirs.

"One day," I said to myself, "I will live differently. I won't treat my children this way. I won't make the same mistakes my parents made." I was wholeheartedly determined *I would not be like my parents.*

.

CHAPTER SIX
THE LIE:

"You're Just Like Your Parents"

*So I find this law at work: When I want to do good,
evil is right there with me.
Romans 7:21 NIV*

There is a debate in scientific circles called *Nurture vs. Nature*. This debate has been raging for centuries. There are scientists who believe we are predisposed to behave in certain ways as a consequence of our genetic make-up. Others argue the environment we grow up in shapes our behavior. For me, I was determined to defy both nature and nurture in my desire to be different from my parents. Everything in me resisted the thought of living life their way.

I rebelled as a teenager, but not like in the same way you typically think of teenage rebellion. My parents partied and I went to church, read my Bible and prayed. My parents dressed to attract the opposite sex, and in my later teens I chose to dress conservatively. I grew increasingly more legalistic and hard on myself. Don't get me wrong, I was not a saint. I made some bad choices and did a lot of stupid things that I regret—I was a kid, but I fought so hard to steer myself in the opposite direction from the path my parents chose. However, no matter how much I resisted, I found myself falling into the same familiar patterns I observed in them—depression, anger, and escapism.

From my earliest memories I recall Dad's battle with depression. His highs and lows, mostly lows, affected the atmosphere in our home and early on I learned not to expect much out of him during a manic episode. Dad grew introspective and seemed deeply tormented at times. Periodically he sat and made groaning noises, or took deep breaths as if he struggled to get air. There were the days of silence and pacing floors. I ached for him, wishing away his pain, but it never helped.

One late morning after a binging weekend, Daddy was overwhelmed with guilt. He and I sat in the quiet of the living room with his head buried in his chest. Suddenly he was crying; a deep, desperate cry. He got up from the sofa and got down on his hands and knees and crawled over to where I was sitting. He put his head in my lap and cried like a baby. He said, "I'm so sorry for what your mother and I are doing to you. Please pray for us, Jamie. Pray, baby."

I stroked his hair like a mother stroking the hair of her child. "It's okay, Daddy. I know it's gonna be okay. I am praying, Dad. I am praying." But it wasn't okay and I knew it. I wanted to scream from the top of my lungs and admit I was falling apart but I couldn't. They needed me to be strong. They needed me more than I needed them, I reasoned.

I was thirteen years old when I recognized my own struggle with depression. I was able to identify what was going on because of the familiar patterns I had seen in my father. I was baffled over my ever increasing inability to manage the sadness.

My own biological changes along with the circumstances of home culminated in an emotional ache that I couldn't shake. I felt myself slipping into dark places I told myself I would never go. Depression is a sadness that doesn't leave. You can be in the middle of an amusement park, outwardly laughing with a group of friends but inwardly crying to yourself saying, "I want to die, I hurt so bad."

I became an expert at disguising my pain. I learned how to put on the James Jeter smile to cover what I was feeling. At thirteen I began begging God to take my life. I fantasized about dying and the relief it would bring. Although I feared the consequences of suicide, at times I fixated on ways to kill myself. I reasoned that if I died then Mom and Dad would stop what they were doing and go back to God—after all it was Demedra's death that opened their eyes to Him in the first place. I reminded God it worked once before, and might work again. "So please take me Jesus," was my constant prayer.

On July 7th of 1979, Mom and Dad were out and I was in desperate pain. I sat down and wrote a letter that I thought might be the last I would ever write.

"Why? Why? Why do Mom and Dad do this to me? They must not love me to do this to me. They must love the bars and things in the world better than they love me. I don't know what I'd do if I didn't have Shannon, Jerry, Tonya, Myla and of course, GOD. I probably would commit suicide.

I never knew what a real good and loving family life was like. I just want them to know that if I ever go to sin it's because of them. Thank you, Jesus for Tonya. She helped me not to go into sin. She said, 'Don't let this ever get you down, O.K.?' I love her very much. Shannon and Jerry, I love them very much. If God should take my life I pray that it causes Mom and Dad to go back into the church and stay there. The reason why I wrote this is because I feel like I'm gonna die. I know it sounds silly but God put these words in my mouth."

On the back I wrote, *"Only open if I die, PLEASE."*

I had forgotten about the letter until more than twenty years later when my mother gave it back to me after finding it among my father's things. I was so young and so broken. I still have it to remind myself of where I was and how far I have come.

As the depression deepened so did the desire to escape any way I could. My mother modeled escapism for me. It seemed as if she retreated into another world and completely forgot her problems and responsibilities.

By nature, Mom was a carefree and fun-loving spirit. She enjoyed a good party and loved to laugh. Board games and card games were among her favorite pastimes. Mom sometimes cooked a huge meal, inviting extended family and friends over for a fun night of games. She was a joy to be around when she was sober.

Quite the opposite of Father, she was the ultimate optimist to offset his pessimism. Mother lived in, what I termed, a Scarlet O'Hara world, "I'll think about that tomorrow." To face the consequences of her choices was just too much for her so she escaped into a world of partying and alcohol. However, when the party was over, there were more regrets. There never seemed to be an end to the vicious cycle.

It was Sunday afternoon and Dad was pacing the floor. Mom was getting all dressed up to go out and party. They slept late into the afternoon after partying two days straight. Mom was chomping at the bits to get back out there. I could tell something was wrong with Dad. He went to the bathroom door and told mother he decided he was not going with her. My heart began to leap within me when he said, "I'm going to church with the girls tonight. I can't keep doing this any more, Mary Ann. It's killing me."

Mom's rancid reply echoed against the closed door, "Well you can go to church but I'm not. I'm going out, with or without you."

Her response came as no surprise to me. When one of them wanted to stop the madness and get their life back on track, the other leaned hard in the opposite direction. They consistently pulled each other back into the mire. My parents were bad for each other.

Dad, Myla, and I, piled into Dad's truck and we went to church while mother headed to her favorite party spot. I was so excited I could barely stand it. Dad was going to church with us! Through the whole service I prayed, "God, please help Dad return to you tonight. Oh God, deal with his heart."

At the end of the pastor's sermon he asked all of us to stand as he gave the altar invitation. I stood praying under my breath for Dad. Suddenly, he leaned over to me and whispered, "Let's go."

"What?" I asked. I couldn't believe what I was hearing, in light of what I was praying.

With a serious and disturbed look on his face he said again, "Let's go."

"What's wrong?" I asked as we headed toward the parking lot.

"I'm worried about your mother. I've got to go get her." he said.

As we pulled out of the parking lot I began to cry. "Daddy, please don't go. You'll start drinking. I know you will."

"No honey. I'm just going to get your mother. That's all."

I was crying hard by now. "You promise?"

"I promise." His terse reply offered me no comfort.

Dad dropped Myla and I off at the house and drove away. I went to the front room window, opened the curtains and sat... waiting. I prayed, I cried, and I waited. I begged God to please make him come back sober. After what seemed like an eternity I saw the car pull into the driveway. For a split second I was elated to see both him and Mother in the car, but as soon as the car was parked I heard the screaming.

I jumped up thinking, "Oh God, he's hitting her. I have to help her." I ran out of the house onto the front porch and saw Dad pull my mom out of the car.

"Oh." I thought, "He must have dragged her out of the bar kicking and screaming. She is mad!" I witnessed Dad's attempt to get her into the house. She was already intoxicated and totally out of control. He pulled her half-way across the front yard, with her fighting against him every step of the way, until he suddenly let go. She fell on her knees in the front yard and lifted her fist up towards heaven and began screaming profanities at God as loudly as she could, and for some reason a drunk can bellow pretty loudly.

"What must the neighbors be thinking? Oh, yeah. They're use to this by now." I mused.

"I hate you God! Leave me alone, God" She yelled between profanities. As she shook her fist towards the heavens, the things she said to God caused fear to grip me.

Dad approached me on the front porch and said, "I'm going in to call Shannon and Jerry. I'm worried about her." Dad told Myla and me to come into the house and leave Mother alone. "She'll come in when she gets ready." Myla and I waited in the living room while Dad made his call and Mom raged in the front yard.

It wasn't long before Mom entered the house. When she came through the front door, I didn't recognize her. I had seen her drunk many times, but I had never seen her like this. She was foaming at the mouth, wetting her pants, screaming uncontrollably and I was afraid. I had never feared Mother before. I had often feared Dad when he was drunk, but Mom never gave me reason to fear her until that night. I decided that eye contact would not be a good idea. I kept my head down and my eyes on the floor. She stomped up and down the room yelling at God.

"Hurry up, Daddy." I thought. I didn't know what to expect from her.

Dad finally entered the room and sat down beside me. "They are on their way. So is the pastor. I've never seen her like this. I'm worried about her." Dad's expression told me in an instant there was more to this than the usual drunken outbursts.

Suddenly, Mom marched over to where I was sitting and stood in front of me. She began pointing her finger in my face pushing me all the way back in the chair and in a low hissing voice she muttered, "I hate you. I hate your guts. I hate you. Do you hear me? I hate you."

I lifted my head and looked directly into her eyes and asked, "Why? Why, do you hate me so much?"

"I hate you 'cause your just like him." as she pointed to Dad. "I hate your father and I hate you."

Dad, trying to ease the pain of my mothers bitter words, said, "Honey, she doesn't mean it. She doesn't know what she's saying."

Everything in me was crushed at that point. The little girl in me was shattered emotionally by those acrid words. The natural part of me that longed for the love of a mother was devastated. But suddenly something supernatural started to happen on the inside of me. My spiritual eyes were opened as I heard my own inner voice saying, "That is not my mother. That is not the woman I remember on the floor of the kitchen enraptured by the presence of God when I was just a girl. That is not the woman who prayed with me when I received the baptism of the Holy Spirit. That is not the woman I would kneel beside just to listen to her pray during family prayer time. That is not my mother."

A holy boldness came upon me and the fear disintegrated. I pointed my finger back at her and said as I looked into her eyes, "I love you. I love you. I LOVE YOU. DO YOU HEAR ME. I LOVE YOU." I was shaking all over. I stood up and pushed her all the way back against the wall. Her entire countenance changed as she stood staring at me. We both stood in silence. Then she turned and began her raging again.

Finally, my sister, brother-in-law, and our pastor arrived within minutes of each other. As they entered, they responded as we did. They calmly sat down and began to pray for my mom who was completely out of control. No one could calm her. Suddenly, she collapsed like a rag doll. At first I thought she had passed out because of the alcohol, but after she fell into the chair she began to weep. That's when the saddest words I've ever heard were spoken out of her mouth.

"I would take off walking, but I don't have anywhere to go. I would kill myself. Oh God, I want to kill myself. But I dread eternity too bad. So where can I go? What can I do?" She wept and I wept with her.

"Mary Ann, you know where you can go and what you can do. You know you can go to Jesus," our pastor gently reminded her.

"I don't want that," she screamed. "Leave me alone."

At that moment, I realized how lost we are without God. Why do we resist the one who has chosen to love us? Why do we struggle and fight Him so? In her effort to escape the pain she only became more enslaved; her questions revealing the utter depths of her personal torment.

As the partying increased, so did the binging episodes. We were left at home unsupervised for longer periods of time. I was fourteen years old when I started driving. I needed to get me and Myla to church, places to eat, school, and wherever children need to go. Mother often left me in charge with a car while they binged. I remember praying the entire time I was behind the wheel for fear of getting caught and because I simply didn't know what I was doing. My courage to get into the driver's seat was fueled from the many times I had taken the wheel when mom, in a drunken state, swerved on the road. I figured it couldn't be too much harder to have total control of the car.

One time in particular when my mom was so drunk she headed the car toward a tree with her foot heavy on the accelerator, I grabbed the wheel of the car and pulled it back onto the road saving us from sure death, only to be slapped in the face. She began yelling at me as she declared up and down that she knew what she was doing. From my perspective, driving at fourteen was less scary than riding with Mom when she was drunk.

I harbored more and more anger, and grew more and more depressed as time went by. I searched for ways to escape my own pain. Through the daily chaos and the emotional upheaval, I discovered my prayer closet. It became my refuge–my security blanket—a safe haven into which I could escape the turmoil that flowed relentlessly through my life.

When I arrived home from school to find the car missing, it signaled that my parents most likely would not be home that evening. I retreated to my bedroom and shut the door. As praise music filled my private prayer room I would crawl up in my Heavenly Father's lap and bask in His presence.

I often asked the Lord to take me back to that place when I was nine years old and encountered Him for the first time in a supernatural way. I turned my thoughts toward the deep abiding security that came upon me that day—diminishing the constant presence of anxiety by withdrawing into the sanctuary of peace He had established for me. Countless times I felt the Father wrap His arms around me, pulling the ache from my heart. I never wanted to leave. I would take my Bible with me into my prayer closet and God's Word spoke to me every time. I knew God was guiding me directly to the passages I needed at that moment.

"The LORD will perfect that which concerneth me: thy mercy, O LORD, endureth forever: forsake not the works of thine own hands." Psalm 138:8

"The LORD also will be a refuge for the oppressed, a refuge in times of trouble." Psalm 9:9

It became a habit to open my Bible to a Psalm and personalize the words, inserting my name or my most recent desperate problem into the eloquent flow of scripture. My prayer life rapidly developed during those difficult years. My relationship with God was not mature, and was rooted primarily in my selfish desire to have my needs met, but God worked with what I brought to the table. During those early years, secluded in the safety of my prayer closet, I eventually learned to battle the enemy of my soul who was constantly whispering *"There is no escape."*

CHAPTER SEVEN
THE LIE:

"There is no Escape..."

I sink in deep mire, where there is no standing; I have come into deep waters, where the floods overflow me.
Psalm 69:2 NKJV

The foreboding atmosphere at home grew increasingly unbearable. I slipped deeper and deeper into depression which manifested both emotionally and physically. Many afternoons I came home from school going directly to bed and awakened the next morning still in my clothes from the day before. Awakening from deep slumber startled me. I remember those mornings.

I darted out of bed, changing clothes as fast as humanly possible, trying to make it to school on time. The simple act of going from one day to the next seemed unbearably painful. I internalized anger, always looking for ways to escape the turmoil. I spent countless hours curled up in a fetal position trying to displace myself—using my imagination to transport me somewhere else. But reality always hit me hard in the face and I eventually discovered every effort to escape got me nowhere. By now I was fifteen years old and feeling like I was thirty.

One day at school a girl in class pointed out the bald spot on the back of my head. Other kids pushed in, gathering around me to stare and some even peeled into my scalp as she questioned me about why my hair was missing. I wanted to hide but there was no place to run. I fumbled through my mind for excuses, which had become my way of coping. I felt cornered and helpless—and my mind drew a blank. This wasn't like the time when a promiscuous girl in gym class, who had a reputation for getting into clubs with her fake I.D., began "outing" my mother to the whole class.

"Hey Jamie. Saw your mom this weekend at The Green Lantern. She was on top of a table dancing and drunk out of her mind."

I remember the smirk on her face as she told everyone what kind of mother I had. When covering by making excuses didn't work fast enough, I chimed in with rest of the girls and started making fun of my own mother, acting as if she was just crazy that way. I rescued myself at her expense, and that carried a certain amount of shame all it's own. But this time the unwanted attention of my peers was more personal.

I couldn't laugh this one off by redirecting the butt of the jokes to my mother. I was completely humiliated. I escaped to the restroom to get a close look in the mirror and was horrified to find a patch of complete baldness. "Oh God. What's happening to me?" After school that day, I begged to visit a doctor immediately.

"There's something terribly wrong. I'm losing my hair, Mother."

Mom drove me to my doctor's appointment. After examination, the doctor called her into the examining room and explained what was occurring physically. He handed a paper with detailed information to both of us while continuing his discourse on hair loss. Finally, he got to the point.

"In other words, the reason your daughter is experiencing this type of hair loss is because she is having a severe mental or emotional breakdown. I highly recommend you get her to a psychiatrist."

On the drive home that day my mom assured me she would get me the help I needed. I remember my response, "No, Mom. God will heal me."

For some reason I thought the news of my breakdown would somehow cause my parents to stop and think twice about their choices and the toll it was taking on our lives, but it seemed my problems were invisible. Nothing had changed. I was under great attack from this point on; emotional, physical, mental, and spiritual. At the age of fifteen, while most teens were enjoying the "normal" ups and downs, I was enduring a nightmare and apparently there was no escape.

My mother and father were so out of control that my friend's parents no longer allowed them to come to our house, it was too dangerous. I isolated more and more each day, stifling my rage and inner turmoil to the best of my ability. Even with all that effort, nothing could prepare me for the spiritual attack I was about to face.

A Wednesday night church service opened the threshold to a personal and furious spiritual battleground. My pastor preached a thought provoking sermon on Jacob's wrestle with the angel of the Lord, and his proclamation, "I will not let you go until you bless me." This intense struggle was a life-changing event for Jacob.

Oh how I desired life-change. I cried out to God that night from the altar. Though the service ended, I was not satisfied. Jacob's proclamation became my anthem. "I will not let you go until you bless me." After the service I retreated to the safety of my bedroom, crying out to God, "Father, I won't leave this place of prayer until I have touched the hem of your garment. I must have change in my life."

I stayed on the floor, my face in an open Bible, for about four hours crying out to God. Around 1:00 a.m. I heard what sounded like a vacuum. It was so vivid it shocked me. Suddenly I was in another realm. I felt overwhelmed by the supernatural activity going on around me. I was frozen with fear. I couldn't move. I heard things that I can't explain to this day, and it was going on all around me simultaneously. I felt an arm rest across my back as if someone or something put its arm around me. I was shaking all over.

I thought, "You've been asking for a life-changing encounter with God and now it's happened but you're scared to death." Something about this didn't feel right, but I was trapped in the experience. My mind raced to the many times in scripture when angels appeared to people and they told them, "Fear Not." But nothing was speaking to me. I was afraid.

I began praying, "Oh God, help me. I don't want to be afraid. Help me, Lord." I knew something was laying on that floor beside me and I needed to see what it was. I turned my head slightly to the right and what I saw looked like something from a nightmare.

A creature that was pinkish-red with leather skin was on the floor beside me. I could see his ribcage and his eyes were huge, his arm draped across my back. He had a mouth full of razor sharp teeth and he was smiling at me. I could sense that he wanted me to talk with him. It was as if he was inviting me into a conversation.

In my mind I was trying to figure out what it was. "Is this an angel? What is this?" The questions were tumbling over and over in my head.

The Holy Spirit began speaking to me and I knew I was not to carry on a conversation with this creature. I began to say, "I plead the blood of Jesus over my life." When I spoke these words, I heard the vacuum sound once again and all the activity in the room ceased. I lay there, curled up in a heap shaking and praying. I knew just as well that there had been angelic beings in that room with me standing and waiting to go to war for me. Yet, the most amazing thing was a little fifteen year old girl discovered her authority that night in the floor of her bedroom. You talk about life-change—although I was confused by the encounter, I believe that God was giving me insight into what victory looked like. I couldn't see it fully then but I would grow to understand it more in the days ahead.

Demonic activity was becoming familiar in our home. There were times when both Mom and Dad had visitations that created deep fear in us. Dad would speak of a creature that stood at the foot of his bed watching him sleep as well as other troubling encounters. Mother had attacks of choking and visibly terrifying spirits. It seemed as if our home was a comfortable place for darkness to play its taunting games and I was a vulnerable target.

The day I collapsed in the entryway of our home after school, something took place in my spirit that I can't explain. I would not be like my aunts. I began fighting off the temptation to believe the lie the enemy was saying to me. That moment was a turning point in the battle for my emotional and physical well-being. At the age of 15, tormented and clinging with desperation to the only answer I knew I could trust, God began teaching me the power of His voice over the voice of the enemy.

The Lord didn't come with a mighty shout, but with a whisper. He gently began to assure me I was going to be alright. I would make it. It was as if he coached me each step of the way. "Jamie, get up from the floor." I slowly made my way to my hands and knees. "Jamie, go call your mother." I crawled to the telephone and dialed the bar that my parents frequented the most. I didn't know what I would say until the bartender got my mother on the phone. As soon as I heard her voice on the other end, I knew the Lord had led me to a point of decision and there would be no room for discussion.

"Mom, I'm moving out." As the words left my lips the burden of hopelessness lifted.

"What?" I could tell from the tone of her voice she'd been drinking although it was mid-afternoon.

"I'm leaving. I'm gonna move in with Shannon and Jerry." I took a leap of faith. I had not discussed this with my oldest sister but I knew I had to get out.

"Well, we'll talk about this later." Even through her slurred speech, her agitation with me was apparent. I was intruding on their party.

"No Mother, there's no need to talk. I'm leaving."

Her tone changed immediately, sensing that I meant to stand my ground "Okay. We'll come home and talk about it."

It was settled. My parents gave their approval. I left home at the end of my tenth grade year. By this time, Shannon and Jerry were living in Niceville, Florida. They welcomed me with open arms, knowing all too well what I was leaving behind. They had accepted their first pastorate position at a small church; for me, it was a place of healing and recovery where at last I found shelter from the storm. I got my first job working at the church's daycare where my sister served as the director. She taught me much and watched over me carefully. Without a second thought, she resumed her role of surrogate mother.

I celebrated my sixteenth birthday just before the big move so the excitement of purchasing my first car helped to push the remaining clouds away that summer. I was overjoyed when my brother-in-law offered to help me car shop and then, with great patience, taught me to drive it. Although I knew how to drive, I'd never driven a stick-shift. With all the enthusiasm of a typical teenager, I embraced every new experience. God had prepared a safe haven for me and I felt my life coming together at last.

I began my junior year at Niceville High School with a deep sense of stability that I had never really known growing up. The turmoil of trying to cope with alcoholic parents and the responsibilities I shouldered for my younger sister left emotional scars, but for the first time they were healing.

I told my sister I wanted to be a hermit at my new school. I was always popular and yet I hated all the pressure that came with it. Even though I detested the attention, my classmates always voted me in for something, and I'd be thrust into the limelight. I might have enjoyed that, but my world was constructed of glass. One stone hurled in the right direction could shatter my fragile existence and I never knew from one moment to the next who might be holding the stone that would do me in—my parents or my friends.

This time I wanted to go unnoticed. I needed time. I needed to heal. I needed to think about my future. I strongly sensed a call of God on my life. The encounter with Him at the age of nine confirmed it to me, but I needed time to seek God for direction. Away from the pressure-cooker of home, I was able to do just that. I spent much time in prayer and in the study of God's Word. One of my favorite passages during this season was Ephesians 4:30-32.

And grieve not the Holy Spirit of God, whereby ye are sealed unto the day of

*redemption. Let all bitterness, and wrath,
and anger, and clamor, and evil speaking,
be put away from you, with all malice: And
be ye kind one to another, tenderhearted,
forgiving one another, even as God for
Christ's sake hath forgiven you.*

I laid this passage before the Lord, bearing my
soul, exposing my deepest agonies to His tender
mercy. I blamed myself for so much, layering guilt
upon guilt. At the same time, the anger I held
toward my parents began to burgeon. The con-
flicted torment of shame, guilt, and anger began
to surface in my time alone with Him. God started
revealing my need to forgive my parents, and
myself. I could not hold onto the past and go forward with Him. His grace to heal my broken heart
could only come through the act of forgiving.

While I was away, my Father worked his way
back to God. Mother was still reluctant and hes-
itant to make the changes Dad was working so
hard to make. I received reports he was hon-
estly trying. But, here again was another way the
enemy would work to keep them in bondage. HE
was working hard yet failing to understand that it
is only by God's grace and not by our works that
restoration takes place.

*I am crucified with Christ: nevertheless I live;
yet not I, but Christ liveth in me: and the life*

which I now live in the flesh I live by the faith of the Son of God, who loved me, and gave himself for me. I do not frustrate the grace of God: for if righteousness come by the law, then Christ is dead in vain. Galatians 2:20-21

One of the biggest lies from the enemy is the lie that we can earn, or work, our way to righteousness. Out of all the deceptive weapons the enemy wielded towards my parents, this one seemed to do the most damage. To accept grace and move forward beyond their past was just too easy—surely God expected more. Yet, the truth is God expects nothing more. When He looks upon those that have repented of their sins, He sees Christ and that's enough, my friend.

The next several months, I dove into my new life and grew stronger each day. I sensed something on the horizon, something God was preparing for me. For months my sister Tonya told me about a young man she met in college.

"You've got to meet Victor Massey" she teased. You are perfect for each other." Little did I know God was at work, orchestrating His destiny for my life.

In a Sunday evening church service God spoke to me about many changes coming my direction. That night the Lord spoke through me and to me by a Word He gave to our congregation. The scripture resounded so loudly:

Trust in the LORD with all thine heart; and lean not unto thine own understanding. In all thy ways acknowledge him, and he shall direct thy paths. Proverbs 3:5-6

I left church that evening, knowing God spoke directly to me and almost immediately I received a phone call from Victor Massey. He asked me out on a blind date. Victor was living in Mobile, Alabama at the time and working as the children's pastor at his father's church. By now, my sister, Tonya, was married and living in Mobile. She and her new husband had just taken a church to pastor across town from Victor's church. They arranged for me to travel the two hours to Mobile to stay with her and we decided to make it a double date.

After just one week of dating, Victor and I were in love. Although Victor and I lived in different cities, the miles could not stop the growing affection we felt for each other. We decided that we would announce our plans to marry on Thanksgiving that year. Victor was so nervous. He had only met my parents once and didn't know how they would respond to our young love.

We spent Thanksgiving in Loxley that year, a small town in lower Alabama, at the home of family friends. I was both anxious and excited about sharing our plans with my parents, but Victor was extremely nervous. The day overflowed with typical holiday excitement; laughter and wonderful food. However, Dad was unusually quiet. I recognized his familiar depression—something was eating at him.

After dinner, Victor asked my parents to step into a room where we could have more privacy. It was the four of us; Mother, Dad, Victor and me.

"Mr. Jeter, I love Jamie and I would like to marry her." My Father stared at the floor. Nervously, Victor spit everything out as quickly as possible and then the room fell uncomfortably silent.

Suddenly Dad began moaning and groaning from the depths of his belly, "Uhhhhhh...Arrhhhhhh...Ugghhhhh..." His sudden painful outburst both embarrassed and alarmed me.

"We're thinking about marrying after she graduates," Victor said apprehensively, not knowing how to react to my father's guttural response.

"I want her to finish school." Dad mumbled, trying to gain his composure.

"Of course, Sir." Victor responded.

Mother began chattering away as if to cover for my father's response. My dad's hands were in his pockets with his head on his chest. Fatigue and agony etched their way deeply into his features. "Be good to her." He said, barely looking up. And with that, we had his consent.

We stepped back into the room with the others, my heart breaking for Daddy. What was wrong? Dad talked intently about death earlier in the day.

He did that at times when he was melancholy, but I knew something was troubling him, something that had nothing to do with the announcement of our engagement.

It was growing late and Victor and I were to drive back to Mobile to spend the next day with his family for the holiday. As I got up to say our good-byes, Dad asked if he could walk me out. Victor left us, knowing we needed a father-daughter moment alone. My father and I walked hand in hand to the car in silence. It was unseasonably cold for lower Alabama, yet at my father's side I felt safe and warm. As we approached the car, he broke down in tears. Weeping, he grabbed me so tight I too began to sob. I needed my Daddy's hugs.

"I want you to come home and live with your mother and I your last year before getting married." He said. "I know you're doing well at your sister's, but I want to spend some time with you—I miss you."

"Okay, Daddy," I wept. "I miss you too." There were more words I wanted to say, but I pushed them back. His emotional state was more than I could bear and at that moment I wanted to console him as much as I wanted to feel the security of my daddy's arms. All these years later, I don't really understand what took place between the two of us that evening as we said our goodbyes. It was a soul splitting sadness I cannot explain.

The tears flowed as we held each other for the next few minutes. Dad kissed me on the forehead and brushed the tears away from my cheek. "Call me when you get to Mobile so I know you made it safely," he whispered lovingly.

"I will."

"I love you, Jamie."

"I love you too, Daddy."

I'll never forget the tenderness in my father's voice when he spoke those parting words. As Victor and I drove away, my weeping grew inconsolable. Even I didn't understand my over-whelming sorrow. "I feel like I'm never going to see him again." I tried to explain, feeling like no one could comfort me at that moment. Little did I know, this was the last time I would see my father alive. The greatest test I had to face was upon me, as I was challenged to question the faithfulness of God. Would I believe the lie...*God is not faithful?*

CHAPTER EIGHT
THE LIE:

"God is not Faithful"

*My tears have been my food day and night, while they
continually say to me, "Where is your God?"*
Psalm 42:3 NKJV

The Friday following Thanksgiving was spent
with Victor's family in Mobile, Alabama. His home
life was such a stark contrast to all that was familiar to me. I navigated through the atmosphere
apprehensively, feeling out of place.

Victor was strong and confident. His parents
had obviously grounded their four children well.
Victor, solid in his faith and commitment to serve
the Lord, was sure of his calling and the direction
his life would take; ministry was his passion. He
spoke often of his dream to be a lead pastor one
day. My vision was to stand beside him in ministry
as his wife. My life seemed to be coming together
at last, and all that God had promised me was
within reach. However, I could have never anticipated the next chapter in the journey.

In the pre-dawn hours of Saturday morning, I awakened to someone knocking lightly on the guest room door. I heard Victor's voice. "Jamie, it's Victor. Can you open the door?"

The intrusion startled me from a deep sleep. For a moment I thought I might be dreaming. Why would he awaken me at such an early hour? "Just a minute" I replied, bolting out of bed to grab my housecoat. I opened the door a crack, still fighting the fogginess of interrupted sleep. Victor stepped into the room, looking a little sleepy himself.

"Tonya and Gary called. They want us to come for breakfast, so as soon as you get dressed we'll head over there." It was still dark outside. The sun had not yet begun to splash color over the early morning clouds.

"Oh, okay" I wasn't quite sure what to think. I heard Victor's parents whispering in the hallway. The whole situation seemed a little odd to me. Victor stepped out of the room and I made my way to the shower thinking to myself, "I'm going to get Gary Taylor for this. He's playing some kind of trick on me."

Gary was like that; a fun-loving jokester at times. It wasn't a stretch to think he must be up to something. I hurriedly dressed, but when I stepped out of the bedroom to let Victor know I was ready to go, his parents were waiting in the den with him.

Victor saw my surprise at seeing them fully dressed and waiting. "Mom and Dad are joining us."

"Oh, that sounds great" I responded, but instinctively I felt like something was not quite right. Victor and his parents were quiet as they drove. I tried to make conversation but the responses were short and the heavy silence seemed foreboding. I was confused, and a little on guard—sort of waiting for the other shoe to drop.

When we arrived at the house, Gary met us at the door. His expression was solemn and his tone, sad. We made ourselves comfortable in the den as Gary walked down the hall to get Tonya. I noticed there was no breakfast, no smell of food cooking.

"What kind of trick is this," I thought to myself.

I heard Tonya sniffling and crying down the hall. "I can't...I can't," she wailed.

"Victor, something's wrong..." I whispered. Finding it hard to conceal my alarm any longer, I rose to go to find out for myself what was going on. Just then, both Gary and Tonya entered the room. It was apparent from their expressions, something was indeed, very wrong. I nestled back into the warmth of the sofa, as Tonya, trembling, took a seat beside me. Victor gently took my hand and his parents moved in closer.

"What is going on?" I thought, searching their faces for an explanation.

"Oh, Jamie. He's dead! Daddy's dead!" Tonya's tearful outburst didn't make sense to me. All that I could think was, *please tell me this is a joke—a sick joke*. I kept waiting, searching their eyes. *Someone please tell me there really is a breakfast and this all a joke!* Tonya grabbed me, weeping. I knew then, it was real.

Gary took a deep breath, hesitating as though the words were too difficult to speak. "Jamie, there was some kind of accident early this morning....and your father... he was killed. We...we don't know exactly what happened yet. I'm so sorry."

Shock washed over me as I looked intently into each face. *Why were they saying this to me?*

"What? You're kidding, right?" I questioned. Momentarily stunned by Gary's admission, my thoughts began to tumble in different directions. Tonya's sobs snapped me into a reality I wanted no part of.

"No...no....no, God...please...no," my own voice sounded strangely distant. Somewhere deep inside, I was screaming—but the scream never surfaced. The tidal wave of emotions sucked me deeper into a chasm of denial. *This could not be happening.* My insides were shaking. I swallowed hard to keep the nausea from overtaking me. I seemed to be floating away as they discussed our next step. Their voices sounded more and more muffled as I withdrew from the horror.

The next thing I remember, Gary, Tonya, Victor and I were in the car driving to Pensacola. Gary had his hazard lights flashing as we raced down the highway to my parent's home. Victor sat next to me in the back seat holding my hand, trying to comfort me but I felt myself slipping away.

All that I had accomplished while living with Shannon and Jerry was stolen from me in an instant. An inch at a time I was clawing my way back from despair, but suddenly, and forcefully, I had been kicked back down into the pit. I felt my fingers slipping from the fragile grasp I had on hope.

Where was God? What about all the prayers I had prayed for my father?

We arrived at my parents home to find cars parked in the yard and all the way down the road. Mom greeted us tearfully as we walked into the house; we never needed each other more than in that moment. Shannon arrived soon after, sobbing in anguish. As the details of my father's death surfaced, it was more than we could bear to hear.

Unbeknownst to us, my brother was in town visiting. Although he wasn't much of a father to him, Dad loved his son. So, when he arrived unexpectedly and invited my dad to a night out on the town, he consented. Mom was at her sewing machine when my father broke the news that his son was in town and he would be meeting him later that evening at a club. She tried to prevent

Dad from going by reminding him how much they had turned things around—they were going to church again, they had been getting their lives back on track. They stopped drinking.

"I won't drink." Dad reassured her. "I just want to spend some time with my son."

"We both know what will happen if we go. James, don't do it," Mother pleaded, but the pull was too strong and my dad would not heed her advice. Mom decided to go with him for fear of the influence she knew this young man might have on my dad. She thought she might have a better chance of keeping him straight if she went along for the ride.

The Friday night after Thanksgiving, they arrived at The Barrels nightclub. It was already late in the evening. As the night progressed, Dad kept his word and decided not to drink. Everything went according to plan at first. They were enjoying the night out, dancing together like old times, and catching up on all the news from my brother. As strong as he thought he was at this point, my dad's resistance finally gave way and he succumbed to the urge to have "just one drink".

Perhaps he thought he could handle one drink and still resist the urge to get drunk. Whatever he was thinking at this point, it was obvious he had fallen for another lie. One drink led to another and mother joined in. Needless to say, before the night was over, they were both drunk. They had partied the night away and the band was leaving. The bar was shutting down and everyone was heading home.

Dad and Mom went out the door a little after 5:00 a.m. As they walked toward their car, they watched a vehicle speed into the parking lot and spin around. My brother approached the two young men in the car as though he knew them. Without warning an argument broke out between the guys in the car and my brother. Dad, out of concern, turned to go toward the car.

Within seconds my brother was wrestling with the driver. The driver pulled a gun and my brother grabbed for it but it went off. The bullet went directly into my father's chest. He was struck in the heart with such force that it knocked him off his feet, throwing him to the ground on his back. Mother ran to him as people screamed, fleeing in all directions. She fell to his side noticing the blood streaming from his mouth.

She leaned in to him screaming hysterically, "James, ask Jesus to have mercy on your soul. Ask Jesus to have mercy, James."

Mother said she could feel it when his spirit left his body. This man was supposed to preach the gospel of Jesus Christ and instead he lay dead in the parking lot of a bar. This anointed man, with a mandate from God, ended life abruptly and violently.

Total chaos ensued as people fled the parking lot fearing they might be next. Someone called for help and within minutes an ambulance arrived along with the police. The paramedics began working on Dad, but could not resuscitate him. "He probably lived two minutes after he was struck with the bullet," one of them said. *Two minutes... Two minutes...*for years after dad's death I set the microwave timer for two minutes just to see how long that was.

After we arrived in Pensacola we were crushed by the horrible details of that night. *Not this way, God. Please!* The enemy of our soul delights in our hurts. He plays by his own set of rules, taking every advantage of these opportunities to kick us when we're down. The questions silently poured through my mind as I pondered God's faithfulness. Had He heard any of my prayers?

The next day the newspaper reported the story of my father's murder. The headlines read "Man Shot to Death Near Area Club" The article went on to say:

> *A man shot early Saturday morning outside The Barrels nightclub, 1096 Navy Blvd., was dead on the scene, according to Escambia County emergency Services dispatchers... One witness, Mark Ramos..., said two men drove into the parking lot about 5:30 a.m. as patrons were leaving the club and began*

to heckle bystanders. The men then aimed a shotgun into the crowd, he said. The gun went off, killing one person; the vehicle then sped away in a southerly direction, according to Ramos[4].

The Sunday morning following Dad's death will forever stay with me. My sisters and I stayed the night with Mother and we all rose to the weightiness of the ordeal. As we sat in the living room, we turned on the television to a regular Sunday morning Christian program. A man sang a hymn that seemed directed toward us.

*How about your heart, is it right with God?
That's the thing that counts today
Is it black by sin, is it pure within?
Could you ask Christ in to stay?
People often see you as you are outside
Jesus really knows you for He sees inside[5]*

We cried together as we felt the presence of the Holy Spirit in our midst. Man looks at the outside, but God sees the heart. It didn't matter what anyone else thought at this point. God alone knew Dad's heart; He knew Mom's heart. He knew all of

---

4   *The Pensacola News Journal; article title: Man Shot to death near area club, Nov 28th 1982*
5   Song Title: How About Your Heat; author unknown

our hearts, and my friend, He alone knows what is in your heart.

Monday evening we attended the viewing. As I arrived at the funeral home, I saw my brother walking up the steps. We embraced each other and wept. I didn't know what to think at this point. My mother blamed him and there were so many questions, but he was still my brother. He was still my father's son.

Victor took my arm as I walked down the aisle to the casket. When I saw Dad's body I was numb. I couldn't cry. I couldn't speak. I just stared. It wasn't real—it couldn't be. He had just hugged and kissed me days before. He had just asked me to come home and live with him before getting married so we could spend time together. My mind blocked everything. I started shutting down emotionally.

"Are you alright, Jamie?" Mother asked as I took my seat next to her on the cold pew. "You don't look good."

"I think I want to leave." I said. "I feel sick." Mother insisted Victor take me back to the house. I was glad to leave—I was so angry. *It isn't fair, God. Things were suppose to get better, God.* That evening was filled with the darkness of my unanswered questions. I think it was the most restless night I've ever known.

Tuesday the funeral was to be held at our home church. The family arrived early and once again

I walked down the aisle to the casket. As we all stood close by, I asked Mother if I could touch him. I needed to touch him so I could believe he was really dead. I placed my hand on his, feeling the cold chill of death. Was it really just a few days ago that we walked hand in hand to the car? How could these cold hands be the same warm hands that made me feel so safe?

"Oh, Daddy..." I sobbed. I leaned over and kissed his head. I can't explain it, but it felt as if he knew I kissed him. Maybe I just so desperately wanted to believe he knew, but for just an instant it felt like he could see me, and I could see him— my real living daddy, not this cold, still form that resembled him.

The church was full. People stood along the walls and the crowd overflowed out into the foyer. I don't know how we would have gotten through that day without the comforting outpouring of love from so many family and friends.

After the funeral we drove to Brewton, Alabama for the burial. Dad always talked about being buried in Brewton. I remember feeling like my insides were jelly as we made the one and a half hour drive. I was trembling inwardly and doing everything I could to hold on to my sanity.

When we arrived at the graveside, I took in the surroundings. I recalled every story Dad told us of his childhood years. I looked at the nearby creek and replayed the stories of him swimming in the icy water. I looked up in the trees and thought of him swinging on the tree branches as a boy, "like Tarzan" he would say. I thought of the old church where he had his experience with God that caused him to walk on cloud nine for days. He grew up in this town with much hope and promise, now he returned in a casket, falling short of all that could have been.

Dad was given a burial with military honors. As the rifles released their ammunition into the air in final salute to my father, my mind raced to Dad's army stories. The soldiers silently folded the American flag that had been draped on Dad's casket and handed it to Mother. I thought of his patriotic love for our country. He would have smiled at such a presentation.

"Daddy, you are worth it." I thought.

After the graveside service we went to our vehicles. Arrangements had been made for us to go to my dad's sister's home. Aunt Margie still lived in Brewton. Food had been prepared for the family by kind strangers. As we drove away from the cemetery, I wanted to scream.

"I don't want to leave you, Daddy. Not like this. Not this way." I needed to be alone. I needed to ask—no, scream my questions to God. Would I ever recover from this?

The voice that taunted me from the past was back. I sensed his invitation to free myself from the pain. *"Let go, Jamie. There's a place on the inside of you that is safe. If you will let go I'll take you there and no one and nothing will ever hurt you again. Just let go of your world."*

The voice of temptation was constant. It sounded so good to be able to crawl inside myself and let go of reality—escape. I wanted to curl up in a fetal position where I could shut out all the pain and protect myself. I could stay cocooned in my own little world forever. Although I knew this was dangerous thinking, I found myself entertaining thoughts of a life within myself. The only way I could fight the voice was through prayer.

"Oh God, I'm in desperate need of a miracle. I'm broken—no, shattered. Is restoration possible and is it for me?"

The Truth

CHAPTER NINE
THE TRUTH:

"God will Restore"

"Restore unto me the joy of thy salvation"
Psalm 51:12 KJV

Not long after the funeral, I began my move back to Pensacola. I packed up my belongings and said my good-byes to teachers, and new friends at Niceville High School. I began the impossible task of emotional preparation. As I geared up to leave my safe haven, I tried to imagine the courage it would take to walk back in to the environment that brought me to the point of a complete emotional breakdown. I had only attended Niceville High School a few short months.

In order to help my mother, I had to return home and re-enroll at the high school in Pensacola. She assured me, if I would quit my job and move back home earlier than initially planned, she would help me financially by paying off my car. She needed me, she reasoned. Under the circumstances, how could I do anything else? I had tasted the difference of life beyond the suffocating dysfunction of home, even if only briefly, and I was uneasy about what lay in store for me there.

As the weeks went by, Victor and I decided to move our wedding plans and marry during the upcoming summer between my junior and senior year of high school. At first mother opposed the decision, but she was so consumed with drowning her pain in alcohol once again, all that mattered to her was her driving need to escape. *Was this why she wanted me home sooner than later?*

Since I was underage, I needed her consent to marry. Surprisingly, she agreed to sign the legal papers for the marriage. Mother dove in to the nightlife hard and heavy, and soon men were consuming her life. Her first boyfriend was in his twenties. He was an abusive addict; the stereo type of the men who would become her pattern for years to come.

Victor and I worked on our wedding plans. That was the life raft that kept me from giving in to the ever-increasing voice of insanity. I made a promise to my father to finish school before I married and I was determined to keep my word, but I needed to get away from my mother's destructive lifestyle. I consulted my school guidance counselor and found that I qualified to get my GED. At that time, Florida law permitted students to take their GED before their class had graduated.

I hashed out a plan for my escape. After I obtained my GED, I could spend the first year of our marriage traveling in ministry with my new husband. If all went according to plan, I could start college the following year. For the seven months prior to our wedding date, I daydreamed about my life as Mrs. Victor Massey. It was a thread of hope that made reality at least a little bearable.

I wanted a big wedding, and I stayed busy with the preparations. After passing my GED, I poured every minute into my wedding plans. Mother had received a decent amount of money through insurance, pension, and other financial sources, as a result of my father's death. Each one of us girls had also received a small financial compensation that my dad had made provision for, upon his death. My dream wedding was going to be expensive, but the finances were available.

Restoration began peeping through the pinholes of possibility. Joy was on the horizon as I dreamt of my future life with Victor. I needed my wedding to reflect hope, confirmation, and promise of a future.

From a young age, I knew I would be involved in ministry; this was the life God created me to live. I knew the Lord had called me, at the age of nine, to share His truth. Working side by side with my husband, I anticipated the many opportunities God would bring our way. In spite of the ongoing drama that played out continuously in our home, my engagement was declaring the truth of full restoration over me. I didn't know for sure how it would happen for me. I couldn't see when I would be rescued from my inward pain, but I knew weeping endured for the night, and joy would come in the morning (Psalm 30:5). I clung desperately to this truth. It was the small sliver of light in my otherwise dark world.

Our June wedding was lovely, and for a 17 year-old, it was a fairytale come true. Victor was so handsome. Almost six-foot tall, dark brown hair, dark brown eyes, with a deep olive complexion. He took my breath away in his white tuxedo. I wore an antebellum wedding gown with a long flowing train. My bridesmaids were beautiful in their wine-colored gowns, each on the arm of a dashing bridegroom in a black tuxedo. Victor's father performed the ceremony. We would be blessed by God, and blessed by family; I just knew it. Victor and I were both very nervous about the life-changing commitments we were making, but we knew God had brought us together; we placed our future entirely in His hands.

The reception made local news. A reporter doing a segment on June weddings asked to interview me, and take pictures of the wedding. The reception was held at a place called The Garden Center. Our friends and family gathered to celebrate the joy of our new life together. After the reception, we drove away through showers of rice and a downpour of good wishes.

In the whirlwind of lace and flowers, cheers, and laughter, I watched my mother waving reluctantly in the distance. I had mixed emotions as we left. On one hand, I was thrilled to be starting a new life with the man of my dreams, but on the other hand, I was sad to leave behind my unstable mother and my precious younger sister, Myla. What would become of Myla?

The early months following our marriage were exciting, yet full of adjustments. Although the restoration and inward healing I longed for was in progress, I still struggled daily to recover the "joy of my salvation". You see, there was a secret I was hiding from everyone in my life.

I was still flirting dangerously with the temptation to lose my sanity. I secretly fantasized of a life void of people. This was so prevalent in my daily existence that it had become sin to me. This form of escapism started immediately following my father's death. I thought by marrying Victor, I could flee the inner torment. I thought my new husband would be a knight in shining armor riding in to rescue the damsel in distress. I needed him to be my savior—to rescue me from my thoughts.

My prayer life changed dramatically during the months following my father's death. I was angry and confused, and my grudge against God grew heavier by the day. I was afraid to pray because I knew I was transparent in His presence—He could see my heart. He knew how I felt towards Him. I repeatedly told myself that I was really mad at the devil because he caused all this to begin with. My spirit was trying to preach me out of the depths of my sorrow and confusion yet, deep within—secretly; I blamed God for everything. After all, He could have prevented all of this, if He chose to, *right?* In the midst of all that inner conflict, my solution was to avoid prayer all together.

During this time, God's voice grew more and more distant. I could no longer hear His voice as clearly as I once had. In hindsight I understand, that in my sin, I became deaf to His voice. In my deceived state, this just gave me more fuel for the fire. Rather than examining myself, I placed the blame on God—sure that He had turned away from me. I became adept at constructing excuses to avoid prayer. Instead, I nursed my anger and stroked my bitterness. I harbored unforgiveness toward God, my parents, and myself. I felt justified in my feelings. Giving my angry thoughts such complete reign over my mind, I entered a dangerous stage of idolatry without knowing it. I no longer sought God as a source of refuge.

I liberally sacrificed at the altar of bitterness. I offered my thoughts to the anger, allowing it to overtake my focus, my faith, and my fellowship. My anger and bitterness became high places to me. A high place is simply anything that exalts itself above God in your life. My inner turmoil was the central focus of my life.

High places originated out of man's desperate need to meet with God before there was a tabernacle or temple. Men of God, like Enoch and Noah, sought out elevated places such as mountains and hilltops to bring their sacrifices in hopes of hearing from God. God always showed up with fire. These high, holy places became a point of reference for generations as people were reminded of the God who spoke to their forefathers. However, as time went on, men began to worship the place, over the God of the place.

Cultic objects and relics were set up in the high places, and eventually became the focus of their worship. High places soon became a place of great idolatry as lewd sexual practices, child sacrifice, and other disgraceful rituals were conducted to their man-made gods. It became easier to avoid Jehovah by going through a set of religious regulations than to engage the one true and living God. Perhaps they too, were afraid that God would condemn them for their sin, if they sought to truly hear His voice. Mankind has practiced avoidance of God for generations, and I fell right into line with many that preceded me.

In First Kings, chapter 3, King Solomon begins construction of the temple and the wall around Jerusalem. The scripture says in verse 2, *"The people, however, were still sacrificing at the high places, because a temple had not yet been built for the Name of the LORD"* (NIV). However, with the temple completed, the people had a place to offer their sacrifices to the one true and living God. But, Solomon began to intermarry with foreign women who worshiped strange gods. This would lead to his downfall as he too began the practice of worshiping false gods in high places. This displeased the Lord so much that the scripture says in First Kings 11:11 (NIV), *"So the LORD said to Solomon, "Since this is your attitude and you have not kept my covenant and my decrees, which I commanded you, I will most certainly tear the kingdom away from you and give it to one of your subordinates."*

Whenever we allow high places to remain, it always leads to division. As I allowed the high place to remain in my life, my soul was divided in allegiance; there was a tearing at the kingdom of my heart. Who would I trust? Who would I believe?

Solomon's son continued in the avoidance of God, worshiping at the high places. King Rehoboam ruled over the Southern Kingdom of Israel and the scripture says, *"They also set up for themselves high places, sacred stones and Asherah poles on every high hill and under every spreading tree"* (1 Kings 14:23 NIV).

King Rehoboam allowed the practice of gross idolatry, and this angered the Lord. King Shishak of Egypt attacked Jerusalem. Through this example we see that when high places are permitted to remain we give our enemy a legal right to mess with us. We set ourselves up to fall under attack. As I continued to fortify my false belief system by justifying my pain, I unwittingly opened the door for great demonic attack and demonic activity in my life.

For King Rehoboam, the attack didn't open his eyes to his sin. He continued to walk in defiance toward God, and the enemy continued to steal from the people of God. King Shishak came into the temple and stole the gold shields made by King Solomon. These gold shields represented a time of prosperity in the nation of Israel. They were symbols of their strength, power, and fortitude. After the king of Egypt stole them, Rehoboam made bronze shields to replace them—a cheap imitation of the stolen treasure.

People are tired of showing up in our churches, at our holy places, only to discover our rituals—cheap imitations of real worship. When high places are allowed to remain, a form of godliness without power takes root in our lives, robbing us of God's genuine power. For me, I was good at going through the motions. Although I was crying out in desperation on the inside, religion made it possible for me to look free—even when I was in bondage. How often do people put on a mask of gold, but inwardly wear a face of bronze. This becomes a high place to us.

One king after another came and went, while the practice of idolatry continued. The scripture says, *"In the ninth year of Hoshea, the king of Assyria captured Samaria and deported the Israelites to Assyria."* (1 Kings 17:6 NIV)

In verses 11 and 12, we discover why the nation was taken into slavery by the Assyrians. *"At every high place they burned incense, as the nations whom the LORD had driven out before them had done. They did wicked things that provoked the LORD to anger. They worshiped idols, though the LORD had said, 'You shall not do this.'"*

High places always lead to captivity. For me, the emotional enslavement I experienced, permitted the adversary to torment me to even greater degrees. At times I balled up in a fetal position, sucked my thumb, and temporarily forced myself to cash out mentally to escape the pain. I usually came to my senses in a river of tears. Weeping awakened me from the prodding, antagonistic voice of the devil. *Help me, God. Please! I'm losing myself.*

The truth is, deliverance comes when we begin to tear down the high places we have allowed to remain in our lives. For Israel, finally, a king with a heart for God came on the scene. King Josiah was just eight years old, but he loved God, and sought to follow after His ways. When he was twenty years old, he ordered a clean-up project in the temple. As the priests were clearing away the rubble, they came across a scroll. When they read the contents of the scroll, they tore their clothing as great sorrow over their sin consumed them. They took the scroll to King Josiah, and upon hearing the law, Josiah took action by ridding the nation of the high places.

"And [Josiah] brought all the [idolatrous] priests out of the city of Judah and defiled the high places, where the priests had burned incense, from Geba to Beersheba [north to south], and broke down the high places both at the entrance of the Gate of Joshua the governor of the city and that which was on one's left at the city's gate." 2 Kings 23:8 (Amplified Bible)

There is only one way to deal with high places in our lives and that is to destroy them. We must become so dissatisfied with the destruction they cause us that we are willing to let go of their imaginary defense, and destroy the control they exert over us. Paul said it this way, *"Casting down imaginations, and every **high thing** that exalts itself against the knowledge of God…"* (2 Corinthians 10:5).

As the nation of Israel cleansed itself of the high places, God restored her peace and prosperity. When I began to address the high places in my own life, restoration was within sight. The truth of God's Word started coming alive to me when God used my husband to speak truth into my life, clearly and boldly.

The truth is, God is a faithful Father and He had not abandoned me in my weakness. Through His truth, I found God making a way for me to combat the lies of hell, and be set free. The truth was, God was working in unseen ways through many sources to teach me His power over worry and fear. The truth is that God wanted me to have lasting deliverance. It was not just a possibility. As I delved deeper into His truth, I wondered, *would God deliver me?*

CHAPTER TEN
THE TRUTH:

"God is a Deliverer"

"For great is thy mercy toward me:
and thou hast delivered my soul from the lowest hell."
Psalm 86:13 KJV

As newlyweds, we lived in Birmingham, Alabama on an old denominational church campground. Several acres, it was centered around a large tabernacle used for the yearly camp meetings and other events hosted by different churches. The denomination's headquarter offices, as well as houses owned by various people (retired ministers and pastors, some of which were rented out by their owners), were also located there. Victor and I rented an old white, wood framed two-bedroom house with black trim. As I remember, it had a small bathroom between the two bedrooms, a cozy living room and an adorable, old-fashioned kitchen. It was our first home, and I was more than excited to begin decorating. I was anxious to place our beautiful wedding gifts in our humble home, and begin working to make it our own little haven.

The area where we lived was riddled with crime and our front door lock didn't work properly, so we propped a chair under the door handle at night. We didn't care—we were too in love to notice any inconveniences or feel threatened by anything outside of our own little world. I would have lived in a mud hut if that's where Victor Massey was. I wanted to be with him, and I wanted to be a part of the ministry God called him to.

For the first six months of our marriage Victor evangelized, mainly preaching in churches across the state of Alabama. It was our sole source of income. We often stayed with people, sometimes strangers, in their homes—which was a huge adjustment for me. I was able to learn from some precious women of God during those months, many of whom poured their wisdom and experience into my life. Finally, Victor was offered a position as Music Pastor/Associate Pastor at a church in Birmingham. We were thrilled with his new job. It offered steady pay, and a place to develop our leadership gifts. About the same time, I was offered a job as the receptionist at the denomination's headquarters. I gladly took it to help with the monthly bills, excited to see God providing for our new life together.

The pastor's wife at our new church became a trusted mentor to me. She often spoke at women's events and I traveled with her, learning all I could. I felt a burning desire rising in me to do what she was doing. I knew one day I would be bold enough to speak into the lives of others and encourage them the way I saw her doing. She also mentored me on how to be a loving wife to my new husband. She and her husband shared the deepest of bonds, evidenced by the respect they showed one another. I wanted the kind of marriage they had. I longed to learn how to treat my husband the way she treated hers. She spent a great deal of time with me and often spoke the truth, in love. When I vented my frustrations and concerns about our marriage, she encouraged me, and gave me godly counsel. It was a wonderful place for us to grow and develop.

Victor was my example of strength and confidence. He never seemed to worry. He was never afraid, or depressed. This was a different way of life than I was accustomed to. I never saw him pace the floor with anxiety—never heard him utter a word of doubt or fear; never witnessed a day of gloom or sadness. He was as steady as they come, and his relationship with God reflected something I had never witnessed; it was genuine. He was not double-minded, but solid in his commitment.

As I saw the Word of God being lived through him, something began to break loose on the inside of me. Daily, the Word of God became life to me. It wasn't just head knowledge, but it became heart knowledge. Words such as, *"Therefore I tell you, do not worry about your life..."* (Matthew

6:25 NIV); and *"Who of you by worrying can add a single hour to his life?"* (Matthew 6:27 NIV), *"Do not be anxious about anything..."* (Philippians 4:6 NIV); or words like, *"And I will restore to you the years that the locust hath eaten..."* (Joel 2:25); and, *"He heals the brokenhearted and binds up their wounds."* (Psalm 147:3 NIV) started leaping to life in my spirit.

Jesus explained the power of truth one day, when He was talking to a group of people. He said, *"And ye shall know the truth, and the truth shall make you free."* (John 8:32). It isn't just truth that sets men free, but it is the knowing or understanding of truth that brings freedom to mankind. I have counseled with many people through the years that have been in discipleship programs, who can quote scripture, and make declarations of faith over their life and yet they are still bound. Freedom comes when the knowledge of truth impacts the whole person. When this occurs, the fallow ground within us is loosened; enlightenment occurs, and revelation produces life.

The day this enlightenment of truth filled my being was a day of freedom I will never forget. I was at home, alone. Victor was going to be gone for several hours, and I was working around the house. I could sense the love of Father God permeating my being all day; I felt overwhelmed by the nearness of His Spirit. As I walked from the bedroom into the living room, it was as if God was waiting for me there. It was truly a divine appointment.

The tangible presence of God was overwhelming. I knew that God Himself, had come to deliver me. I stood in awe of Him; speechless. I lifted my hands in adoration and fell before Him on my knees. With tears streaming down my cheeks, I worshiped Him. I had not worshiped Him so freely in a very long time. Suddenly, from the depths of my being, I released a shout. I surprised myself, as the sound of my own voice reached my ears. Like a dam breaking loose, the waters of shame, guilt, pride, self-righteousness, deception, came gushing forth. I took a deep breath and another shout came forth and with it depression, fear, anxiety, anger, worry—heaviness drained out. I continued to shout and the walls of my emotional confinement continued to crumble.

Like Joshua and the children of Israel shouting at the walls of Jericho, something supernatural ignited on the inside of me. Every barrier to freedom had to fall before the Lord my *Deliverer*—the enemy could no longer be at home in the territory of my mind. Suddenly, with the release of another shout, I saw a dark figure as it came off my back and shot out through the ceiling of the house, fleeing in terror. The spirit that had oppressed me for years could no longer taunt me. Like the children of Israel coming out of Egypt, nothing would hinder the day of my deliverance.

My provision for freedom had already been bought and paid for by the precious blood of Jesus Christ. I was not meant to remain a slave in my Father's house. I was created to live in the abundance of Sonship. The high places began crumbling as the truth roared to life inside me.

In Genesis, chapter 38, we read the story of a woman by the name of Tamar—an unlikely candidate, destined for position and blessing. She had married into the household of Judah, the son of Jacob, and into a lineage of promise. God promised his great-grandfather, Abraham, an unprecedented blessing that would extend throughout generations.

Tamar had married the firstborn son of Judah which meant that the blessings would fall upon her own firstborn son. Unfortunately, there were some small obstacles standing in the way of her future blessing. Her husband died and left her childless. She married his brother, but he also died leaving her childless.

She was sent to live in her father's house until the third son, Shelah, was old enough to marry her. But when Shelah came of age, he married another woman, leaving Tamar to live out the remaining days of her life as a widow in her father's house. Her basic needs would be taken care of: food, shelter, and water, but she would only be existing. This was not her destiny and she knew it. She knew she had married into the household of blessing, and yet, here she was living out her days as a widow.

Don't you know—every day she arose and put on the widow's garment, she did so knowing this was not how it was suppose to be. *I thought I married into a place of promise. How did I end up here?* I can easily imagine her thoughts; can't you? With each passing day, her widow's garment reminded her that she had nothing to show for her life. The garment represented a life of disappointment, depression, and despair. She was, literally, cloaked in bondage.

One day she received news that Judah, her father in-law, was going to Timnath to shear his sheep. She arose, shedding her widow's garment, and instead, decked herself out in the garment of a harlot. While you might be gasping at her audacity, don't miss this point: Tamar shed her garment of death and put on the garment of conception—life. She was determined to obtain what she knew was rightfully hers. She was willing to risk everything—ridicule, loss, and even her life, all to conceive for the future. She was determined to come out of the barren place, and pursue a fruitful place.

Tamar waited patiently in the shadows for Judah to pass her way. When he finally arrived, she propositioned him for sex. Judah didn't recognize her. Thinking she was a harlot, he slept with her and she conceived. The end result was the birth of twins, and of which one, Perez, is listed in the book of Mathew in the lineage of the Messiah.

Tamar could have lived her entire life as a widow; her basic needs provided for, but never obtaining the life she was promised. Instead, she chose to pursue an abundant life. Friend, the abundant life is ours to pursue. It's time to shed our widow's garments. You and I were meant to produce life!

When the spirit of heaviness left me, I began to rejoice. I laughed so hard, I could barely catch my breath. It was as if someone had told the funniest joke I'd ever heard. I couldn't stop the laughter; and with it, came a deep sense of security and well-being. *Life!* The joy of my salvation returned, just as I'd prayed. Praise the Lord! I don't know how long I basked in His presence, but I knew I was free, and I couldn't thank Him enough. Please hear this, *God is passionate about your freedom.* He has made every provision possible for you. However, you must *choose* to live it. Get up and pursue it!

I walked in the beauty of my deliverance for days. I was alive again. Just like Moses speaking to the Israelites when crossing the Red Sea who said, *"… For the Egyptians whom ye have seen today, ye shall see them again no more for ever."* (Exodus 14:13), I knew this was an enemy I would not have to fight again. My understanding of truth would keep me free.

Although Victor and I were happy where God had appointed us, we could see our limitations and realized the need to further our education. Recognizing our need for development, we resigned our positions at the church. On the heels of much prayer, we decided to move to Cleveland, Tennessee, so we could attend Lee College, now Lee University, in the fall of 1984. The move was right on schedule. A year and a couple months after marriage we placed ourselves on track to pursue God's future for our lives. Victor was returning to his studies and I was just getting started.

We rented a comfy one-bedroom apartment, off campus. Our lives were full of activity as we attended school each day, worked jobs, and traveled on weekends, preaching the Word. Often, our peers thought we were brother and sister; they were surprised when they found out we married so young. I didn't feel young; I had already lived a lifetime in so many ways.

I thought about how Daddy would feel about my decision to attend Lee. Sometimes, I walked the campus wondering if he had walked where I was walking. Even after his death, my father was still very present in my thoughts; I missed him. I constantly had dreams of him, as though he were among the living. In my dreams, he was always smiling. However, I had a deep need to know that he was okay, despite the circumstances surrounding his death. Where was he spending eternity? I asked God to reassure me that he was not suffering. I prayed for God to give me the peace I needed, and He did.

Victor and I traveled to Mobile, Alabama, to visit with Tonya and Gary during school break. One evening, Gary preached at a local church, and Victor went along. Tonya and I remained at the house. We spent the evening at her dining room table talking about Dad, and how much we missed him. We shared our tears, as tender memories poured out. It was then we learned, we'd both been experiencing recurring dreams.

"I just wish I knew where he was spending eternity," I confessed. Suddenly, music wafted through the house; a chime that sounded familiar to both of us. Our eyes grew huge as we looked at each other. Instinctively, we grabbed one another tightly for security.

"Do you hear that?" Tonya's question almost seemed like an echo; as I thought it, she voiced it—it felt like we'd stepped into the twilight zone.

"Yes," I whispered. "Where is it coming from?"

"I don't know," Tonya said, choking back her alarm as we gripped each other closely.

We cried and laughed together, neither of us willing to express fear. We stood up, holding each other, as we made our way through the house to locate the source of the mysterious music. We walked to one side of the house, through the bed-rooms, but the chimes grew distant. We eventually made our way to the to the master bedroom, on the other side of the house. As we got closer, we realized the melody must be coming from a music box.

When we entered the room, Tonya nudged me and pointed to the top of a dresser. On top of the mirrored-hutch was a wind up music box in the shape of an old fashioned church. The music box was playing the song, *Amazing Grace*—over and over again.

Tonya looked at me, laughing while tears rolled down her cheeks. "You have to wind that music box up for it to play. I haven't dusted up there in a long time." We both laughed and cried as we tried to take it in.

"I believe God sent angels to wind the music box over and over again in answer to our prayer, Tonya," I laughed. *Amazing Grace*. We stood there as the music continued playing and basked in the answer to our prayer. *Where was Dad?* The answer; God's grace is beyond comprehension.

My legalistic mind had surmised that Dad had blown it. He ruined his opportunities, and God punished him for it. But in that moment, Father God took on a whole new perspective for me. He was showing me, once again, the depths of his love. God has gone the distance to show His love for us. His grace is overwhelmingly powerful. To try setting limits to it, is humanizing the omnipotent God. His grace is not meant to be fully understood, it is meant to be received.

Amazing Grace, how sweet the sound,
That saved a wretch like me.
I once was lost but now am found,
Was blind, but now I see.

T'was Grace that taught my heart to fear.
And Grace, my fears relieved.
How precious did that Grace appear
The hour I first believed.

Through many dangers, toils and snares
I have already come;
'Tis Grace that brought me safe thus far
and Grace will lead me home.

The Lord has promised good to me.
His word my hope secures.
He will my shield and portion be,
As long as life endures.

Yea, when this flesh and heart shall fail,
And mortal life shall cease,
I shall possess within the veil,
A life of joy and peace.

When we've been there ten thousand years
Bright shining as the sun.
We've no less days to sing God's praise
Than when we've first begun.

John Newton (1725-1807)
Stanza 6 anon.

What a memorable moment. When I left Tonya's house that night, I never again questioned my dad's eternal state. I was able to truly put it in God's hands. The peace that I prayed for, was now with me. I could trust Father God with my dad's eternity—He was gracious. God was turning my mourning into dancing. Every attempt of the enemy to make my life miserable in the past, was only serving to shape my future for ministry.

It's God's way; *what was yesterday's misery is today's ministry.*

CHAPTER ELEVEN
THE TRUTH:

"Yesterday's Misery is Today's Ministry"

Thou hast turned for me my mourning into dancing.
Psalm 30: 11 KJV

Victor and I enjoyed our studies at Lee. We were full-time students, working daily and traveling on the weekends. We watched, amazed, as God worked mightily in and through our lives; it was an exciting time for us. Unfortunately, living so far away from family, I grew increasingly distant from my mother. When I did speak with her, the conversation often left me in tears.

My father's death certainly didn't awaken her to the need for change in the way she was living. Instead, she seemed to be willfully headed on a fast-track of destruction. Her drinking and partying escalated to such extremes that she was rarely sober. The young man that moved in with her shortly after my father's death, didn't hang around long. She soon found another abusive man to take his place.

Mother had many close calls with death. One would think at least one of those close calls would shake her up enough to take stock and turn away from the party life. However, the closer the call, the deeper she seemed to plummet into self destructive habits. I tensed each time the phone rang. The minute I heard the voice of certain family members, and friends of hers, my stomach knotted with anxiety. *Were they calling with more bad news?*

There were also the desperate calls from my mother. Sometimes she was so drunk all she could do was ramble on and on about her internal pain. She was crying out for help on one hand, but she could also be very hateful in her drunkenness, and say horribly painful things that I knew she wouldn't remember the next day.

At other times, Mother called screaming in fear on the other end of the line. I would answer the phone only to hear her voice filled with terror; crying desperately for help. It didn't take much to trigger my old familiar roles: protector, rescuer, enabler.

Although, I moved miles away from her, the triggers remained intact. Each time she called, I instinctively responded—it was my role to rescue and protect her. "Mom, what's wrong? Is someone hurting you?"

I always responded to her panic. She ranted about demons attacking her, describing them and yelling, "Pray, Jamie. Pray!" I tried to get my bearings, but the calls were unnerving. A million questions raced through my mind all at once. *Is she hallucinating from the alcohol? Is she really being attacked by demons?* Prayer is the only thing that seemed to calm her. Once, out of sheer frustration, I handed the phone to Victor to pray. I just couldn't do it.

I began to view my mother as a desperately broken woman that had been ravaged by the enemy. The stories she told of her youth seemed to bring such pain to her. She had been victimized by so many throughout her life. I came to feel increasingly sorry for her.

In Judges 19, we find the story of a woman who was abused so severely that the consequence for her abusers was death. We do not know her name, but the atrocities inflicted upon her so displeased God, that the punishment almost caused the extinction of one of the tribes of Israel.

The story is of a Levite and his concubine. She left him to go back to her father's house. Although the King James Version of the Bible, as well as other commentaries, argue she played the whore (v.2), I believe a more accurate interpretation of the passage reveals she left him because she was angry with him (RSV, NRSV, NEB, BBE, NJB).

There was some sort of domestic battle going on between the two of them, and she tried desperately to find sanctuary by returning to her father's home. The Levite immediately pursued her. He arrived at her father's house and coerced her to return. We can only surmise she felt threatened by him, or knew she wasn't loved. From the scriptures, it is obvious her father tried to protect her and she was reluctant to return with the Levite. However, on the fifth day, late in the afternoon, they saddled their donkeys and began the long journey home. They arrived at Gibeah, in the territory of Benjamin, at a late hour (v.11). They waited for someone to offer a place for them to bed down for the night, but no one was willing to take them in as the darkness encroached. Finally, an old man offered to give them lodging for the night (vs. 16-21).

Suddenly, a band of sexual perverts bent on having homosexual relations with the Levite, came beating at the door (vs. 22). Much like the story of Lot, we see the great sin and apostasy the nation was walking in at this time in history. The Levite confirmed the implied distrust the concubine had for him, by throwing her out to the mob in order to save himself. All night long she was gang raped, brutalized and tortured by the mob until they all had their fill of her. Somehow, this poor woman managed to crawl back to the old man's house by dawn. Due to loss of blood and the severity of abuse, she died reaching the doorsteps of the house (vs. 25-26).

Every time I read this story in scripture my heart breaks for this woman. As I see her reaching for hope, I think of the countless people who have suffered abuse and mistreatment, and never find the hope they reach for.

The Levite opened the door to leave early the next morning, and finds his concubine on the steps. What he does next is just as shocking as his first crime of throwing her to the rabid band of predators—he tries to ignore what happened to her. Stepping over her, he tells her to get up. It was as if he wanted to put it out of his mind, pretending nothing ever happened. When she didn't respond, he knew it was too late. She was dead (vs. 27-28).

People that suffer abuse commonly find those close to them wanting to pretend it never happened. They try to move past it, ignoring the heap of damage lying there, exposed. Often the victim is incapable of speaking about the injustice, because part of them has died. The last thing these hurting individuals need is to be ignored, walked over, disgraced, and not validated. Nevertheless, God hears the secret cries of the mistreated and abused. In love, and with justice, He will deal with the sin—He will not ignore it.

Outraged by what has happened, the Levite decides to send a message to all of the tribes of Israel about the injustice of this horrid act. He dismembers his concubine, cutting her into twelve pieces, and sends sections of her body to each tribe. The tribes were shocked to discover what wickedness had been done to this woman. There had never been such a detestable act committed in all of Israel (vs. 29-30). Instead of the tribe of Benjamin dealing with the sin, and punishing the people responsible, they chose to cover the sin and protect the men involved. As a result, civil war broke out as the eleven tribes go to war against Benjamin. Only six hundred from the tribe of Benjamin survive the war (Judges 20). Destruction and death are the effects of sin, when man chooses not to deal with it.

I saw my mother much like this woman—broken in pieces by the sin that ravaged her. I pitied her and grieved over her pain. I often prayed for her, but I also grew discouraged when she seemed to be getting worse. I grew weary of believing for her deliverance as time wore on, without any signs of hope. There were plenty of times I wrestled with God arguing, *"I can't pray for her right now. I'm struggling to believe, Lord. Will she ever change?"*

One day, as Victor and I were traveling, I received insight from the Holy Spirit on how to pray for her. I was to begin envisioning her as whole. Not a broken woman in a thousand pieces, but whole. I started praying what I envisioned. I saw her once again as a praying woman. I saw her singing the praises of God. I no longer saw what she was, but saw what she would become, once again, when she surrendered her all to God. It was faith in what

I envisioned for her that helped me withstand the choices she continued to make.

❧

After spending a year and a half at Lee, we accepted the lead pastorate at a church outside of Birmingham, Alabama. I was only nineteen years old when we moved from Cleveland, Tennessee to begin our new adventure in ministry. I enrolled at the University of Alabama, Birmingham, to continue my education, but the greatest education of all took place in that small Alabama town.

The church had a reputation of being unable to keep pastors. We knew the challenge was great, but we were so excited that we dove in with all our heart. Victor blossomed during our tenure as lead pastors. The call of God was evident as the shepherding gift activated, and began flowing through him. He was a born leader. People were attracted to his confidence and natural ability to lead and it didn't hurt any that he was a talented singer, as well. The anointing to lead people in worship was especially helpful during those early years when we couldn't afford to hire a music pastor. Our little country church started growing as people received salvation. The fire of revival burned brightly.

A year into our pastorate, I took a job at a day-care center as a pre-school teacher. I enjoyed working, going to school, and being a pastor's wife. One morning, on my way to class, I felt nauseated. I thought I might be coming down with a virus, but this virus wasn't going away. I soon discovered I was pregnant. The day I told Victor was memorable as we anticipated, and celebrated, the birth of our firstborn. Due to my increasing morning sickness, I couldn't keep up with my classes and had to drop that semester. I continued to teach up until the end of the school year.

The nine—almost ten months I was pregnant with Micah, I dreamed about the healthy environment my son would be raised in. He would never have to fear or wonder what his night would be like. He could enjoy being a child without living in the shadow of guilt and shame. He would know the safety and security of two parents who loved God with all their heart and loved each other unconditionally. I knew the hand of God was on this child. I sensed his heart for God. Even while I carried him, his life spoke volumes to me.

My mother came one week prior to my due date with the intention of assisting me after the birth of my son. I was two weeks past my due date when the doctor decided to induce labor. I could tell Mother was getting antsy and needed a drink. By this time, she was a straight vodka drinker and couldn't go very long without getting the shakes.

A few days before being induced, Mom was exceptionally jittery—she was trying to find a way to prepare me for her departure. I let her off the hook when she started making excuses about why she needed to return to Pensacola. I let her know I would be fine, if she needed to leave. She stayed around a couple of days after I came home from the hospital, doing what she could to help. I sensed her agitation, and was more than ready to say thank you and goodbye by the time she left.

I was twenty-one when Micah was born. We lived in a parsonage next door to the little church we pastored. It was a wonderful place for Micah to explore and enjoy those early years, and I thoroughly enjoyed my role as a new mother. I spent my days pouring into my son. I started teaching him the principles of scripture while he was just an infant. I purchased flannel-graph bible stories and we had daily bible studies together. I was teaching him how to pray and spend time with the Lord before he could even carry on a conversation. I modeled it before him—I was committed to my time with God and did not hesitate to bring him into my prayer closet.

As much as I enjoyed my role as mother, wife, and pastor's wife, something was still missing. I knew the call to share God's Word was on my life. The stirring of the Spirit of God was strong, and I knew there was more in ministry to come. Victor asked me to speak on Mother's Day, and I was leading bible studies in our church. These opportunities were fulfilling, and I knew this was a foretaste of what God had in mind for me.

One day, as I was traveling down a winding country road close to home, the Lord began revealing greater understanding of this call on my life. It was a warm, sunny winter's day. The trees were bare; the grass still gray. Micah was in his car seat fast asleep, and I was enjoying the view as I drove. The sun beating down on the glass was heating the car up, and my heavy sweater made it so warm that I considered rolling the window down.

"Lord, if I didn't know better, I would think it was Spring time," I said lightheartedly.

As soon as the words left my mouth, I heard the Spirit of the Lord say to me, "Jamie, even nature knows how to discern its season. It's aware that more winter will follow. It understands that if it blossoms today the winter will bring death to its beauty. So, it is content to wait for its season." That was a wonderful revelation to me. I knew God was letting me know I would have days that felt like Spring, but the fullness of what was to come, in His call on my life, would require waiting on Him.

From that point on, I was content to walk in the season I was in. My role as mother, wife, and pastor's wife, were all part of my preparation. My greatest calling was to be a good wife to my husband, and a nurturing mother to my child. The season for the pulpit ministry would come in His time. As I accepted God's timing, more revelation into what God had in store was unfolding for me. I knew I would be raising up praying priests—men of God—and I must not take my role lightly. This was my highest priority.

However, moments of Spring did come, just as the Lord promised. I started getting invitations to speak at women's events. When I received the first invitation, I put out a fleece before the Lord. Much like Gideon in scripture, I asked the Lord for clear confirmation. I needed to know if it was truly God calling me to go and share His Word. I know there is much debate about whether we should put fleeces before the Lord, but I was in desperate need of confirmation.

I accepted the invitation to speak on a Wednesday night, at a women's service an hour's drive from our church. I prepared my message. I knew I was to share some of my own personal testimony. To speak of my own struggle and to be so transparent was terrifying but I sensed the divine leading of the Holy Spirit. I asked the Lord to give me souls. I prayed earnestly and expectantly, "Let someone come to you for salvation, oh God. This will be the confirmation I need to continue walking in this new direction."

I was trembling the whole drive over, and more so after I arrived. As I awaited my introduction,

I was sure everyone could see how terrified I was. But something started to happen as I stood behind the pulpit. When I opened my mouth, the anointing of the Holy Spirit flooded me and I knew I was not ministering out of my own strength, but through the unction of the Holy Spirit.

As I shared just a portion of my testimony, healing and freedom went forth. God took the misery I suffered, and used it to bring deliverance to others. When I gave the altar invitation, many came forward for ministry. I didn't ask if anyone needed salvation. Yet, as I began to minister to individuals in the prayer line, a precious young lady asked to accept Christ as her Savior. I knew God was revealing to me His master plan. No experience would be wasted; *it was part of the purpose of God for my life.*

CHAPTER TWELVE
THE TRUTH:

"God Has a Purpose for My Life"

For I know the plans I have for you," declares the LORD,
"plans to prosper you and not to harm you, plans
to give you hope and a future.
Jeremiah 29:11 NIV

The opportunities for me to speak began to increase. As much as I enjoyed every service, seeing lives changed as I shared my testimony and taught God's Word, I also knew I had to be obedient to my highest purpose first—as a wife and mother. One of my mentors shared some wise advice with me that I now pass on to others.

She had taken a few days away to seek the Lord for direction. She fasted and prayed, and yet, after three days had not heard anything from God. She was packing her things to get ready to go home when she finally heard the Lord say, "What would it profit you to gain the whole world but lose the souls of your children?"

When she shared this with me, and a few others sitting close by, it was an arrow of wisdom that struck me directly in the heart. Micah was just a baby, and the invitations to travel and share God's Word were starting to come more frequently. Although I wanted to say yes to every invitation, I knew the Lord was issuing a warning to be obedient to follow His voice, and timing, as His purpose continued to unfold in my life.

By this time, I was teaching Sunday school, and serving as president of our women's ministries, as well as director of our music program at church. I took Micah with me to every practice and every meeting, exposing him to the joy of ministry as much as possible. I refused to let these activities infringe upon my devotion as a mother and wife, but I also saw each opportunity as part of Micah's development. He loved the house of God. As just a toddler, I saw the worshiper arise within him. He loved to sing and was sensitive to the moving of the Spirit of God. I knew my responsibility was huge to help him tap into this gift and funnel the flow of the anointing on his life properly.

When Micah was two years old, I became pregnant with my second son. While carrying him, I could sense the fire of God within him. With Micah, I knew he had a tender heart for God, but this child possessed a blazing zeal for God and I knew it. When I was six months pregnant, I was asked to speak at a women's service in Tennessee. After praying, I knew I was to take this appointment.

I began my scripture study in preparation for that evening. As my spirit quickened to the Word the Lord was giving me, I could sense the child in me also stirring. I imagined this was a small taste of what Elizabeth felt when carrying John, the Baptist. As I delivered the Word to the women that night in Tennessee, I felt like a woman on fire. People told me they had never seen me minister with such boldness. I told my husband afterwards, "This child has fire in him. I can feel it."

The day our second son was born, we had not settled on a name for him. But the moment he was delivered from my womb he released a cry that startled everyone in the delivery room. He was a large baby and his voice was deep and loud. He came forth like a bold lion. We decided to name him Caleb Joshua. When they placed him in my arms, I began to prophesy over our new son. "You are Caleb Joshua. You will fight giants and you will win."

As my children grew, I would often say to them, "No matter what you choose to grow up and do with your life—doctor, plumber, businessman, minister—your profession will always take a backseat. It's not what you do, it's who you are. You are first and foremost a man of God. Don't ever forget it."

I enjoyed my children. As a woman, I felt the greatest gift God had given me was that of mother and wife. My purpose would be fulfilled with even the day-to-day activities involved with these roles. However, the enemy tried to make me feel I was ignoring my calling because I was not moving full steam ahead into the pulpit ministry. Eventually,

I understood the source of much of this pressure came from the mentality of the culture.

During the 1980's and 1990's, the pressure for women to have it all, and be it all, was immense. To me, it seemed that society measured success by your ability to juggle your household, career, and personal life with perfection. Women who were bread-winners, with perfect bodies and spotless homes became the model. However, from my perspective, the children of our postmodern era were getting the short end of the stick. They were the afterthought for many women.

The mantra of the hippie era of the sixties and seventies was *"if it feels good, do it."* I could attest that many children who were neglected as adults pursued what "felt good" to them: sex, drugs, and rock-and-roll. The product was a generation that grew up to become self-centered individuals. The 1980's were plagued by greed and a driving force to be number one. Although the pull to buy into this way of thinking was strong, I knew what had been revealed to me concerning God's purpose for my life. So I had to keep this before God in prayer on a daily basis, and intentionally choose to rebel against the mindset of a generation.

Lest it appear that I'm putting down those whose purpose was to build a career while raising a family, let me clarify. Because I am the type of person who pours my all into whatever I'm doing, the ability some have to balance it all, I lacked. By my own convictions, I had to continue to follow what God was revealing to me personally in order to align myself with His purpose for my life.

Jesus had to confront a selfish mentality, much like our present day, when the disciples began coveting positions of authority in His kingdom. They asked Him in Matthew, chapter 18, "Who is greatest in the Kingdom of Heaven?" Jesus placed a child in the center of them and began teaching a lesson on self-abandonment. We start to get some insight to the heart of Jesus for children—and for us all. He continues with a stern warning:

"And whoever receives, and accepts. and welcomes, one little child like this for My sake, and in My name, receives and accepts and welcomes Me. But whoever causes one of these little ones who believe in, and acknowledge and cleave to Me, to stumble and sin [that is, who entices him or hinders him in right conduct or thought], it would be better (more expedient and profitable or advantageous) for him to have a great millstone fastened around his neck and to be sunk in the depth of the sea. Woe to the world for such temptations to sin and influences to do wrong!" (Matthew 18:5-7 Amplified Bible).

Although this passage is referring to spiritual children, I believe we can hear the heart of God concerning our natural children as well. To welcome—that is, to invest into the lives of our children—is an investment made into the Kingdom of God. But to offend (hinder in right conduct or thought) our spiritual or natural children is a serious offense against God.

The mentality of the world is bent on negatively influencing our youth. Thus, the assignment to raise godly children became my passion. I desired more than anything else for them to know Father God. I would take the wisdom I had learned through much hardship and pour it into their lives. I could see how my testimony was more than just for a congregation of many; it was for an audience of little Massey's.

I may have learned this from my mother. I recall many times her saying it was her purpose in life to give birth to us girls. She found meaning in the lives of her five daughters. I often reflected on this when carrying out my role as mother. Watching Mom's life taught me so much—even the things that brought pain. As an adult, I was still witnessing and learning from the effects of her choices.

Late one night we received a call. Mother was in the hospital because her live-in boyfriend put her there. In a drunken stupor, he had beaten her severely and her jaw was broken. She needed surgery to wire her jaws shut as the break healed. The recovery time would be extensive. He could have killed her.

Mother was recuperating during the Christmas holidays. We all met at Tonya's house that year for the festivities. My mother's lifestyle was catching up with her and taking a toll on her health. She had been diagnosed with type 1 diabetes in her forties. She was playing a dangerous game with her life each time she drank alcohol and took insulin shots. Yet, even a disease would not stop her strong drive for the addiction. Her eyes looked hollow for more reasons than one—the weight loss, the addiction, her health, but most troubling of all—the spiritual deadness.

These years were filled with the consequences of her destructive choices. She had been arrested for drunk driving one too many times. Her license had been revoked for five years. Although she was forced to go to Alcoholics Anonymous by the court system, she hated it, and got nothing from it. We tried rehab but she would either check herself out of the rehab center, or be asked to leave for various reasons. She was restless and relentless in her addiction. I wondered what it was going to take to turn the situation around.

Mom had lost her way. She was aimlessly wandering through life searching for meaning. Like many in her situation, she couldn't find any purpose for living. Much has been said about discovering our purpose in life. This is not a new revelation. Jeremiah understood the importance of grasping his purpose.

"Then the word of the Lord came unto me say-ing, Before I formed thee in the belly, I knew thee; and before thou camest forth out of the womb I sanctified thee, and I ordained thee a prophet unto the nations." (Jeremiah 1:4-5)

It was the accepting of his purpose that car-ried him through the difficulties he would face as a prophet to a rebellious nation. He prophesied purpose to the nation of Israel when God spoke through him declaring, *"For I know the plans I have for you," declares the LORD, "plans to prosper you and not to harm you, plans to give you hope and a future"* (Jeremiah 29:11 NIV). God had a big purpose in mind for the nation of Israel despite all the bad choices they made. He used Jeremiah to remind them of this truth.

The truth is, we were created for the sole pur-pose of bringing glory to God with our lives. The enemy has always worked to stop us in our pur-suit, in order to hinder the increase of God's glory in the earth. But God has chosen to use every experience of our lives to give satan a black eye. The good, the bad, and the ugly—God can bring purpose out of it all and bring glory to His name.

God Will Use the Good
He chose to work through the good to fulfill His purpose as in the case of a man by the name of Abraham.

"Abraham believed God, and it was counted unto him for righteousness. He staggered not at the promise of God through unbelief, but was strong in faith, giving glory to God" (Romans 4:3; 20).

He chose to work through the good as in the case of a man by the name of Joshua. Joshua was mentored by Moses. He was faithful to believe God when the majority doubted they could take the land.

"Have not I commanded thee? Be strong and of good courage; be not afraid, neither be thou dismayed: for the Lord thy God is with thee withersoever thou goest" (Joshua 1:9). Joshua's life was marked by great victories as God used him to lead the nation into Canaan.

God Will Use the Bad

God chose to use the bad to fulfill His purpose as in the case of Joseph. He was rejected by his brothers, unjustly convicted of a crime he did not commit, and spent many years separated from the father he dearly loved. Yet he came to understand, "Even though you intended to do harm to me, God intended it for good, in order to preserve a numerous people, as he is doing today" (Genesis 50:20 NRSV).

God chose to use the bad as in the case of Stephen. He was a man full of the Holy Spirit, and was divinely used of God in the early church. But

he was falsely accused of blasphemy, and stoned
to death. As he was dying he said, *"Lord, lay not
this sin to their charge"* (Acts 7:60). A man by the
name of Saul was a witness to his death and, I
believe, a recipient of Stephen's prayer for grace.
Saul would later become Paul and go on to write
most of the New Testament.

God Will Use the Ugly

God will use even the ugly moments to bring
about his purpose as demonstrated in the lives of
David and Bathsheba. It couldn't get much uglier
than this. Their adulterous one night stand led
to the murder of Bathsheba's husband, and the
death of an innocent child. Yet, we see the depths
of God's grace when David said to Nathan, the
prophet, *"I have sinned against the Lord. And
Nathan said unto David, "The Lord also hath put
away thy sin; thou shalt not die"* (2 Samuel 12:13).
From David and Bathsheba would come Solomon, Israel's greatest King.

In the life of Peter, we again see God turning
around some rather ugly moments. Peter followed
Jesus throughout His earthly ministry, and vowed
to stand by His side regardless what came their
way. But when the moment presented itself during
the trial and crucifixion of Christ, he failed to keep
his commitment, showing his true colors as profanities accompanied his denial of Christ. It was the
ugliest, lowest point of his life.

After Jesus' resurrection, he appears to Peter and assures him that his purpose had not ended. *"He saith unto him the third time, Simon, son of Jonas, lovest thou me? Peter was grieved because he said unto him the third time, Lovest thou me? And he said unto him, Lord, thou knowest all things; thou knowest that I love thee. Jesus saith unto him, Feed my sheep" (John 21:17).* Peter came forth with more determination to fulfill God's purpose for his life. On the day of Pentecost, with boldness, he proclaimed salvation and three thousand people were converted.

Nothing is Wasted

Too often people want to sweep the bad and the ugly experiences of life under the carpet. We can't see how God can do anything with the pain of poor choices or unjust treatment. We would just as soon put these things in a place where we no longer have to deal with them. We only want the things we are proud of to be visible. Yet, the Apostle Paul said,

But God has chosen the foolish things of the world to put to shame the wise, and God has chosen the weak things of the world to put to shame the things which are mighty; and the base things of the world and the things which are despised God has chosen, and the things which are not, to bring to nothing the things that are, that no flesh should glory in his presence" (1 Corinthians 1:27-29 NKJV).

If people look at our lives and see *us*, we have fallen short of our purpose. But if people look at our lives and see the miracle of Christ in us, than we have fulfilled our purpose.

Freedom would continue to flow through me as I shared, with transparency, my own battles and victories. I wanted my sons to know James Jeter, although they had never met him. It was important that they learn from his life the way I had. I wanted them to see how I responded to my mother's addiction; I didn't hide the frustrations, hurt, and embarrassment. I wanted them to learn from my own mistakes. I knew they would, but most importantly, I wanted them to understand that God can bring purpose out of our pain. Understanding this would serve to equip them, as it had me, to discover and walk out their own unique purpose—*God equips the called.*

CHAPTER THIRTEEN
THE TRUTH:

"God Equips the Called"

For God has not given us a spirit of fear, but of power and of love and of a sound mind.
2 Timothy 1:7 NKJV

For almost six years Victor and I pastored the church outside of Birmingham, Alabama. The church, our children, and ourselves were in a constant state of growth, and the continuous changes meant a lot of stretching—physically, emotionally, and spiritually. The steady growth of our church family finally overwhelmed our tidy little building so we launched a building project to provide ample space.

God had given us our dream—to go to a city and continue building a ministry that would bring glory to Him. We were satisfied in the work He called us to, and we envisioned ourselves planted at this church until retirement. I wanted my children going through all twelve years of school in Birmingham, but God had another plan.

When the Lord started dealing with our hearts about new places, we initially resisted. I thought surely this must be the devil trying to get us to abandon our dream. Yet, the Lord continued dealing with us, eventually helping us get to the place emotionally where we could let go, but it was not easy. We were more than ready to leave when the time came, but the bonds we made with friends over so many years, and the emotional attachments to our home and our church, were painful to sever.

The day we packed the moving truck and said our good-byes was heartbreaking. I waited until everyone left the house and I walked through one last time. As I entered the boy's vacant bedroom, my mind raced to all the cherished moments we shared together in that room. I stood and wept, feeling like the dream I once held for them—to know the security of growing up in one place—was lost. I went to each room crying in self-pity over what I was giving up in obedience to God. I finally made it to the den and fell down on my knees weeping. My heart was grieving over unfulfilled dreams. But the Holy Spirit began reassuring me; He knew exactly where he was taking us. What He had in store for us would far outweigh what I thought I was losing.

Victor didn't have clear direction on where we were to go. We decided to move our family into a little apartment close to Victor's parents and from there, we would evangelize. Although we had complete peace about the decision, we also knew it would not be easy. Unlike the first time we traveled preaching the gospel, now we had two small children to take with us. I was concerned about how this would affect their lives—always in different churches and staying in the homes of different people. But God used this time to prepare us for the destiny He had already charted for all of our lives. After a year and several months we eventually moved back to Cleveland, Tennessee where Victor finished his education. I took this time to pour more of myself in to my children.

One day we received a call from a man in Wichita, Kansas asking us to consider a job as the denomination's State Youth and Christian Education Directors. We would also work to help plant new churches throughout the state. Although this was quite a distance from home, we knew we were to take this bold step. We began making plans to relocate our family and ministry.

After Victor graduated, we moved to Wichita to begin our new venture. We served the churches in Kansas for two years, during which time God was equipping us with more administrative skills, as preparation for greater ministry responsibilities that were ahead. I have learned to embrace God's equipping process. I must admit at times I have resisted, but I've learned the process is better than being unprepared for the next step. According to the dictionary, the word *equip* means to furnish with intellectual or emotional resources—to prepare.

The Equipping Process

First, we are often *uncomfortable* as the equipping process begins. Things change all around us. Like a mother eagle preparing her eaglets for independence, God will make the nest an unpleasant place to live. Sometimes it's a stirring from within, other times it's external pressure and sometimes times, it's both.

As a child growing up in the panhandle of Florida, I lived in a highly populated military area. There were times when military war games were played between the soldiers and you could hear planes flying overhead and gun fire. The soldiers talked about dreading "the games." For various reasons, most of them didn't enjoy this type of training—fighting one another. However, the training was necessary. It equipped them to be good soldiers and prepared them for war. War games, much like boot camp, were uncomfortable but it served to prepare and equip them for the challenges they would face on the battlefield.

David had to endure the discomfort of living in caves as God prepared him to take his position as King over Israel. Yet, some of his most meaningful psalms were written during this season of his life. Being uncomfortable is counter-cultural; we live in a society that constantly seeks the easy life. However it equips us with patience, endurance, and readiness.

Secondly, the *unknown* can be quite challenging in the equipping process. God spoke to Abraham to leave the familiar and go to a place he had never seen before. *"By faith Abraham, when called to go to a place he would later receive as his inheritance, obeyed and went, even though he did not know where he was going."* (Hebrews 11:8 NIV). Stepping into the unknown requires faith and trust. This is often the greatest area of battle within us because our mind wants to rationalize and, thus, convince us how ridiculous it is. If we are willing and obedient we learn how to discern the voice of God.

Thirdly, the *unusual* is realized as we are equipped by God. Peter experienced the unusual when, by faith, he walked on water.

"*During the fourth watch of the night Jesus went out to them, walking on the lake. When the disciples saw him walking on the lake, they were terrified. "It's a ghost," they said, and cried out in fear. But Jesus immediately said to them: "Take courage! It is I. Don't be afraid."*

"Lord, if it's you," Peter replied, "tell me to come to you on the water." "Come," he said. Then Peter got down out of the boat, walked on the water and came toward Jesus." (Matthew 14:25-29 NIV).

This was humanly impossible and totally irrational. Yet, Peter chose to listen to the voice of

Jesus, and by faith, he experienced something supernatural, divine, and completely unusual. It is this part of the journey we do things we never imagined. This is also where we experience our greatest opposition from the enemy. We have to encounter the waves, wind, and boat dwellers for the unusual to be realized. But if we remain focused we will move into the final phase of the process.

The end result of the equipping process is realized as we are *unleashed* into the activation of our call. We will find doors opening, a time of soaring, and a release to operate effectively.

The first century church witnessed this as God equipped them to take the gospel into all the world.

*"They devoted themselves to the apostles' teaching and to the fellowship, to the breaking of bread and to prayer. Everyone was filled with awe, and many wonders and miraculous signs were done by the apostles. All the believers were together and had everything in common. Selling their possessions and goods, they gave to anyone as he had need. Every day they continued to meet together in the temple courts. They broke bread in their homes and ate together with glad and sincere hearts, praising God and enjoying the favor of all the people. **And the Lord added to their number daily those who were being saved."** *(Acts 2: 40-47 NIV, emphasis added).

Many signs and wonders were done through the church, and the result was the birth of the greatest movement in history as they were unleashed. What the Lord had promised, they were living.

For Victor and I, the equipping process was well underway as we dove into our new calling in Kansas. Part of Victor's responsibilities as the State Youth Director was to organize youth camps for children during the summer. The camps consisted of daily fun activities and church services in the evenings. Our second summer, Victor asked if I would be the speaker for one of the weeks of camp. I enthusiastically accepted the offer only to struggle later. I found the more speaking I did, the greater attack I would have. It was the same old cycle and it was getting familiar to me, but I was tiring of the harassment. I came to the place where I dreaded each speaking appointment. It was always the same. A constant intimidating badgering from the enemy followed every invitation.

"Who do you think you are?" the devil would say. I struggled and fought the intimidation until the moment I walked into the pulpit; but then anointing would come and I would move in confidence as the operation of the Holy Spirit flowed through me. As soon as the service was over, I would step out of the pulpit only to experience the intimidating voice of the enemy again. Soon I was isolating and fearing invitations.

The week arrived that I was to speak to the kids. I had prepared countless hours in study and prayer. Victor helped me set up the stage the night before the camp was to start. We worked late into the evening with our young sons at our side. We finally went to our cabin and I settled the boys in their beds. Everyone had fallen asleep. I laid there staring at the ceiling, hearing the all-too-familiar taunting voice of intimidation. I eventually drifted off to sleep and experienced a spiritual dream that forever changed my life and ministry.

In my dream, I was walking down a dark, wide, dirt road. The path was lined with woods on each side. For as far as I could see, ahead or behind, there was nothing but road in sight. I remember wondering how I got on the road. I didn't know where I was headed, but I felt if I kept walking forward I would eventually land at my destination.

Suddenly, I heard footsteps in the distance behind me. I turned around and saw a man on the road. Recognizing that it was just the two of us on this dirt road, I was a little concerned. I didn't know the man, and had no idea why he was following me, but I didn't panic because he was a distance behind me. I decided to pick up my pace a little to make sure I stayed ahead of him, but I could hear him getting closer. My heart started beating faster as my fast walk became a jog, then a run. With each stride, I heard him closing in on me. I was now running as fast as I could possibly run, yet he was on my heels. That's when I noticed he was laughing at me. I turned to look at him and his face was distorted and evil. I knew his intentions were to rape, torture, and kill me—totally violating me. He was close enough to grab me, but instead he stayed on my heels running in stride with me, laughing the whole time.

"Oh God, save me," I cried out, in my dream.

I heard the Lord reply, "You can rise above him."

"How?" My question was filled with desperation.

"Believe!" The Lord shouted. I started to believe I could rise above him, and I did. I rose above him, yet both of us were moving at a fast pace. He was still running below on the road, and I was above him. By now he was jumping up trying to grab and pull me down. I was growing weak, starting to sink.

The Lord yelled, "BELIEVE!"

I started to believe and I began to rise again. Then I heard the Lord proclaim, "Hit him. Hit him on the head."

I took my hand and hit the man on the top of the head. As soon as I struck him, his head began to bobble. He looked disoriented and stunned, but he shook it off and came right back leaping and laughing at me.

Once again the Lord shouted, "Hit him again! You have the power to hit him on his head."

I took my hand and hit him again on top of his head. Like before, he was disoriented, but he shook it off and came right back at me again leaping and laughing. His laughter was more than I could bear.

I finally cried out, "If he will stop laughing, he can have me."

At that moment, I sat straight up in the bed weeping. Opening my eyes, I could feel the presence of the Lord in the room. I heard the Lord say clearly, "Jamie, you have battled the spirit of intimidation long enough."

The Lord immediately set me free from the power of intimidation. It was then I realized, this too, was a battle that my father fought. He had allowed intimidation to consume his confidence, robbing him of his calling.

My father carried a great anointing during those times in his life when he was submissive to the Lord, and walked in his calling. However, the deep-seated feelings of unworthiness that he carried always led him back to his old ways, and straight into the arms of the enemy.

Like my father, I was falling into the trap of comparisons. Whereas my father would measure his holiness to that of others, never feeling he could measure up to their standard, I was hard on myself—a perfectionist that failed to meet my own standards.

The apostle Paul was clear about the danger of comparisons. *"For we dare not make ourselves of the number, or compare ourselves with some that commend themselves: but they measuring themselves by themselves, and comparing themselves among themselves, **are not wise.**"* (2 Corinthians 10:12). Paul was saying if a person's standard is always themselves, or if they compare themselves with one another, they are without understanding.

Jesus battled the spirit of intimidation in the wilderness. He was faced with the challenge of recognizing who he was. The enemy tested Him with the "if you are" trap. *"If you are the son of God"* (Matthew 4:3,6) the devil said, *"then prove it"*. Yet, the Heavenly Father Himself had just declared Jesus, forty days earlier, as the son of God.

And lo a voice from heaven, saying, "This is my beloved Son, in whom I am well pleased." (Matthew 3:17)

The enemy was tempting Him to question what God had already declared over Him at His baptism. When we don't understand who we are, we fall into the comparison trap. The sole purpose of the comparison trap is to stop our assignment.

Each of us has been given an assignment by God that He has equipped us for.

"For we are God's workmanship, created in Christ Jesus to do good works, which God prepared in advance for us to do." (Eph 2:10 NIV)

The Apostle Paul said we all have an assignment to do good works. God spoke your assignment in advance of your arrival; it was spoken into eternity. He has made provision for your preparation. The enemy understands this, and works to hinder God's purpose from coming forth in our lives.

In Ezekiel's vision of the valley of dry bones, the prophet saw the death of the assignment of the nation of Israel. They were in Babylonian captivity—talk about intimidation. Would they ever return to Israel? The nation had a huge mission given to them by God. They were His chosen people. Out of this nation would come the Messiah, the Savior of the world, and the enemy was after their assignment.

We see, in Egyptian bondage, the enemy's attempt to oppress the assignment. We see, during the time period of the Kings, an attempt by the enemy to confuse their assignment. When we get to this passage in Ezekiel, we see a time when the enemy would seek to destroy and kill the assignment of Israel.

As Ezekiel gazed out into a valley of dead, dry bones the Lord asked him, *"Can these bones live?"* (Ezekiel 37:3 NKJV). Ezekiel replied, *"O Lord GOD, You know."* God's instruction to Ezekiel was to prophesy—declare—over the bones, *"You shall live!"* (Ezekiel 37:5-6 NKJV). As the prophet spoke truth over the bones, suddenly death took on life.

A great army rose up from the dust and fulfilled their assignment.

Friend, sometimes you must declare over your assignment, "You shall live!" God has made it possible for you to fulfill your destiny. This assignment is bigger than you. It's about generations that become recipients of the fulfillment of God's promise on your life. God has equipped each of us with what we need to accomplish our assignment.

Through the revelation of scripture, words spoken from God to me through dreams and in prayer, I came to understand that my assignment *must live*. I refused to fall into the trap of comparisons, and I refused to allow intimidation to rob me of my destiny. I saw how the enemy tried to destroy my parent's assignment, and I refused to end up a casualty—I would be the conqueror that Jesus died to make me. As I declared with boldness over my assignment, *"You must live,"* I was free to soar unleashed—*the curse was broken.*

CHAPTER FOURTEEN
THE TRUTH:

"The Curse is Broken"

Christ redeemed us from the curse of the law...
Galatians 3:13 KJV

When Adam sinned against God in the garden, mankind fell under the curse of the law which resulted in poverty, sickness, and spiritual death. This poverty was more than just financial bondage; it also involved poverty of the soul which is the mind, will, and emotions. Poverty effects mankind on many different levels. Yet, when Christ came He redeemed or bought back our complete freedom, and the curse was broken. However, one of the more clever ways the enemy has worked in the lives of God's people is through the blinding of our eyes to the full freedom that we have in Him.

Godly people struggle to live daily in the security of liberty purchased by Christ. Jesus declared in Luke 4:18, *"The Spirit of the Lord is upon me, because he hath anointed me to preach the gospel to the poor; he hath sent me to heal the brokenhearted, to preach deliverance to the captives, and recovering of sight to the blind, to set at liberty them that are bruised."*

Christ liberated us once and for all from the oppression ushered in through Adam and Eve's encounter with sin.

2 Corinthians 3:17 says, *"Now the Lord is the Spirit, and where the Spirit of the Lord is, there is liberty."* The word *liberty* in the Amplified version of this passage is interpreted as *emancipation from bondage.* So, why are God's people living as if they are still under the curse if we are redeemed? Although we have touched on the subject of freedom in previous chapters, let's explore more closely some hard facts that keep people from finding their freedom in Christ. First, we don't know who we are.

The Hard Facts
We're not fully grasping our identity in Christ. YOU ARE HIS!

This unrecognized truth played a key role in my mental anguish through the years. Although I knew I was in relationship with God, I failed to fully understand my privileges as a daughter of the King. It was easy for the enemy to talk me out of joy, peace, and confidence when my identity was wrapped up in my environment, my accomplishments, and my failures. Lest we forget—it is not who we are, but whose we are. There has been much written and said on this subject over the years, yet we still struggle with understanding our identity in Christ.

In 2Corinthians 1:21-22, the Apostle Paul says, *"Now it is God who makes both us and you stand firm in Christ. He anointed us, set his seal of ownership on us, and put his Spirit in our hearts as a deposit, guaranteeing what is to come."* This passage holds crucial keys to understanding our identity in Christ. We must grasp this! These truths are the gateway to transformation from a life lived in bondage, to experiencing the fullness of freedom God intended us to live.

❖ **Truth One:** you are firmly planted in Christ. *"Now it is God who makes both us and you stand firm in Christ. (v.21)* Although your world may be turned upside down, your feet will not be moved. You are safe.

❖ **Truth Two:** you are anointed. *"He anointed us..." (v. 22)* There is yoke- destroying anointing upon you. Regardless of how the enemy seeks to bind you, the anointed One in you has given you authority to destroy the enemy's yoke. The anointing is a God-given power that renders us effective, but it must be activated.

❖ **Truth Three:** you are sealed by The Holy Spirit and hell sees His stamp of ownership—*legal right of possession* upon you. *"...(He) set his seal of ownership on us..." (v.22)* Since you are possessed by God, the enemy doesn't have a legal leg to stand on, against you.

❖ **Truth Four:** the Holy Spirit in you, is God's guarantee for the fulfillment of all His promises—both in this life and the life to come. *"...and put his Spirit in our hearts as a deposit, guaranteeing what is to come." (v.22)* You must personalize these truths in order for them to work for you.

This is not God's Word for a select group, but to *all* that are saved. Another way the enemy keeps us from freedom is through ignorance.

Ignorance: Spiritual blindness to our bondage.

John 12:40 relates how the religious people of Jesus' day missed the hour of His visitation partly due to spiritual blindness. *"He has blinded their eyes and deadened their hearts, so they can neither see with their eyes, nor understand with their hearts, nor turn—and I would heal them."* We must pray and ask God to reveal any areas of bondage we are ignorant of, or blinded to. Sometimes our hearts deceive us, and in ignorance we accept the oppression of the enemy and even equate it with God's will for our lives. Turn, allow the Lord to heal you—it's His will.

Allowing circumstances to control our thinking

Often, we fix our eyes on life's events allowing circumstances to dictate our decisions. If things are going well we interpret it as God's goodness gravitating toward us. We're doing everything right, we surmise. If life is challenging and trials are mounting, we extract from our circumstances that we must be doing something wrong or that God is angry with us. The enemy works hard to keep our circumstances within the line of natural sight so that our faith is removed, and doubt invades our thought life. We allow financial situations, health issues, job security or insecurity, marital and family problems, to dominate our lives.

Once again, the Apostle Paul gives us the best advice on how to live above our circumstances in Philippians 4:7-9 AMP. *"For the rest, brethren, whatever is true, whatever is worthy of reverence and is honorable and seemly, whatever is just, whatever is pure, whatever is lovely and lovable, whatever is kind and winsome and gracious, if there is any virtue and excellence, if there is anything worthy of praise, think on and weigh and take account of these things [fix your minds on them]. Practice what you have learned and received and heard and seen in me, and model your way of living on it, and the God of peace (of untroubled, undisturbed well-being) will be with you."* We might entertain the notion that this way of thinking is living in the realm of denial. "I'm a realist" we argue. But this is not the realm of denial, this is the realm of truth—it is where the God of peace abides. Finally, sin keeps us enslaved.

Confession of sin leads to freedom

Colossians 3:5-6 tells us, *"Mortify therefore your members which are upon the earth; fornication, uncleanness, inordinate affection, evil concupiscence, and covetousness, which is idolatry: For which things' sake the wrath of God cometh on the children of disobedience."*

The Apostle Paul was speaking to Christians in this passage. In much of this chapter he spends his words to urge believers to give themselves completely to Christ. In verse 5, he lists several sins that must be put to death or they will take us back into bondage. Un-confessed sin reopens the door to the curse we have been redeemed from, and I'm convinced, is the root of most of our torment in life. We will never be at peace if we are habitually sinning and not allowing the Holy Spirit to deal with our sin. Daily cleansing in prayer is necessary and will enable us to walk as spiritual, rather than carnal, believers.

Although there are other obstacles that can stand in our way of complete freedom, we must remember there is emancipation from bondage. As I grew in the knowledge of this powerful truth, I discovered freedom more fully in my own life. Liberty was growing steadily in every area.

After our two-year tenure in Kansas, we moved to Northern Ohio where we served for four years.

These were great years for our family and we enjoyed our experience immensely. It was during this time the Lord brought much needed closure to unresolved issues from those early years. I was sharing my testimony often, and each time it brought greater healing to me—it was therapeutic. I wanted to make sure my family was comfortable with my transparency. Out of respect for my mother, I called her before each speaking engagement to get her blessing. She was always so proud, and my sisters were supportive and prayerful. I am eternally grateful for their encouragement since this was my personal key to greater freedom.

Each one of us has a story to tell; a story that will touch the heart and lead someone to the same freedom. The enemy wants to silence our stories because he understands the power of our testimony. *"They overcame him (satan) by the blood of the Lamb and by the word of their testimony"* (Revelation 12:11). I witnessed this power as many came to Christ and received deliverance and healing as a result of God's redeeming truth in my story. However, I longed for the day I could share my mother's restoration and I prayed earnestly that the curse she was under would no longer hold her prisoner. *What would it take, Lord?*

Mom had been through much and had faced death on several occasions, but she still had not hit bottom in her addiction. The Holy Spirit, however, was working on mother's heart, and tenderly continued to draw her.

In the story of the prodigal son (Luke 15:11-32), the young man had to reach a point of realization and desperation. You would have thought the loss of wealth and the pain associated with wild living would have been enough to turn him around. Yet, he had not hit bottom. A severe famine hit the country and he was in dire need. Possibly this would cause him to turn and change. He had still not hit bottom. He was seeking employment in the most degrading places and was content to accept a job working with pigs. You would think he would have come to the realization before ever showing up his first day on the job to feed pigs, *something has got to change*. But, he still had not hit bottom. It was only when he reached into the pig slop to fill the deep hunger in his belly that his eyes were opened and the scripture says, *"...He came to his senses" (v.17 NIV)*. He finally hit bottom. As a result, he went back to his father's house and there was great restoration and celebration. I couldn't imagine, after all Mother had been through, what it would take for her to hit bottom. However, God knew and mother was about to "come to her senses."

Mother's older sister lived in Denver, Colorado and my mom loved her dearly. She and her sister favored each other in looks, and seemed to be closer to one another in affection. One day mother received a call that her sister was dying of Cirrhosis of the liver. Like Mother, she battled alcoholism for much of her life.

Mom caught a plane to Denver to be with her sister in the closing hours of her life. When she arrived at the hospital and walked into the intensive care unit she was overwhelmed. Mother said when she entered the room and saw my aunt, it was like looking at herself. She stayed close to her bedside for the duration of her illness, singing at times to comfort her. Although my aunt was unable to speak, she was alert. Mom said she could see the fear in her eyes. Mother didn't want to die with fear in her eyes. She didn't want to die this way at all. It was her wake-up call.

After my aunt passed, Mother returned home. She began examining her life and where she was headed. By this time, her heart was being drawn back to the truth that she once walked in. She began, as she called it, "wooing the Spirit of God." This was her way of saying she stopped avoiding the loving voice of God and started drawing near to Him again.

My brother-in-law, Gary, was preaching a revival in Pace, Florida which is approximately thirty minutes from where Mother was living. She decided to attend one of the services. God dealt with her throughout the preaching of the Word, and when the altar invitation was given, she responded. That night she returned to God and was gloriously set free from addiction. She never returned to alcohol and didn't suffer the effects of withdrawal; it was a supernatural deliverance.

In the past, trying to stay sober was impossible for her but what was impossible for her, was possible for God. She was ready to leave behind the addiction and the curse of sin was broken—it could no longer hold her captive. The prison the enemy constructed for her demise, had to release her. When she fully submitted to Christ, His blood was enough to break the stronghold of addiction and free her from the chains of its misery.

Mother immediately began making changes. There was true repentance as she moved forward with joy into all that God was restoring to her. She had a live-in boyfriend who was good to her, but she wasn't interested in marriage. She let him know she could no longer live in sin and he moved out. She stopped going to familiar places and cut her ties to her former life.

The woman I had envisioned as whole and set free through those difficult years of addiction and torment, was now coming forth. Only God can produce such radical change. She was my faithful prayer partner every time I traveled and spoke. She had heard me share my testimony, and would cover me each time I was asked to share it again. She knew how difficult it was for me, and I'm sure it was difficult for her to hear. But she would often say to me, in so many words, "It's your testimony.

If it will help someone else, then tell it." Now when I shared the story, I was able to speak of God's delivering power in mother's life. Her story was weaved into my story, creating a beautiful tapestry that declared the glory of the Lord.

Ohio was a place of God's restoration on many levels for me. One night I had a dream of my brother whom I had not seen since Dad's funeral. In the dream, he called me crying. I asked him what was wrong and he kept saying he was sorry. He said, "I killed your dad. I'm so sorry." I awakened from the dream and began weeping.

A few days later, my sister called informing me that a national talk show had contacted her because they were doing a show on second chances. They said our brother had called asking them to find his sisters so he could ask for a second chance. They were asking us to appear on the program to talk about what happened when my father was killed. My sisters and I decided this was not the forum to discuss what happened. After we declined, they asked if it would be okay if our brother contacted us, and we consented.

Soon I received the call, much like my dream. God had prepared me in advance. My conversation with my brother brought healing for both of us. My brother was attending church and turning his life around. The curse that had plagued our family for years with pain and disillusionment was being shattered, and the enemy of our soul was being defeated. I believe God delights in the open show of humiliation upon the enemy. "*And having disarmed the powers and authorities, he made a public spectacle of them, triumphing over them by the cross*" (Colossians 2:15 NIV).

When we fully embrace redemption and live accordingly, it disarms the enemy. God has already broken the curse through the cross, but it is still a choice that we make daily—to walk in the fullness of the blessing. I've come to understand our choices are critical; *our choices truly do effect eternity.*

CHAPTER FIFTEEN
THE TRUTH:

"My Choices Effect Eternity"

*This day I call heaven and earth as witnesses against you
that I have set before you life and death, blessings and curses.
Now choose life, so that you and your children may live*
Deuteronomy 30:19 NIV

God is all about choices. Both privilege and responsibility are inherent in the choices we make. God knew, before He created mankind, we would abuse our privilege and not take our responsibility seriously; so *He* made a choice. Before God ever set creation into motion, He made a decision to provide a way for us to have a relationship with Him, and He did this considering the impact of man's negative choices.

"According as he hath chosen us in him before the foundation of the world, that we should be holy and without blame before him in love: Having predestinated us unto the adoption of children by Jesus Christ to himself, according to the good pleasure of his will." (Ephesians 1:4-5).

In the garden, man made a terrible choice that ultimately led to the change of his environment, his lifestyle and his relationships. One choice altered everything. However, through divine election, God offered salvation to everyone, everywhere. He determined beforehand that He would accept all who choose salvation, adopting them into His family. Because of His redemptive plan, we now have the privilege of restored fellowship with God and others. However, the choice is ours alone; and it is obvious mankind still struggles with making responsible choices that lead to life and not death.

Although for years Mother's choices were leading to death, the day she decided to return to her first love (Revelation 2:4), was like spring returning after a long winter. Joy and peace adorned her as my mother delighted in her restored fellowship with God. Our relationship blossomed like flowers in May. I enjoyed calling her on the telephone and having conversations about God. I will forever cherish the time we spent regaining what was lost to sin for so many years.

During this time of renewal between my mother and I, other changes were taking place as well. Victor and I keenly sensed a new season approaching for us. We both felt a strong desire to return to the pastorate. We had served the churches in Northern Ohio for four years and our tenure there was coming to a close. It was at this time the opportunity to pastor a church in the Atlanta, Georgia area opened for us. After praying, we knew it was the right place to plant ourselves for the next season.

Atlanta is a growing, multifaceted city; diverse in every way. It was fertile ground for our budding ministry and the perfect place for our children to develop their gifts. We grew to love the city with all its challenges and conveniences. So many of my prayers, prayed even as a child, were answered through our ministry in the ATL-Atlanta. We embraced many nationalities as our multicultural church family blossomed. As a young girl, God seeded me with a deep desire to reach the nations. Each service, as I glanced across the sanctuary I saw the nations united in one Kingdom, and my heart leapt with joy. God never forgets our prayers.

One of the benefits of living in Atlanta was the short driving distance to Pensacola. It is approximately a six hour trip, which proved to be a blessing in disguise in the coming years, as Mother's health began to fail and she needed us more and more. My mother was very independent which, at times, made it challenging to help her.

My sisters and I were scattered throughout the country from Los Angeles to Atlanta. We tried to go down periodically to clean her house; sometimes taking turns or meeting together in Pensacola to take her to doctor's appointments or assist her recovery through many different surgeries. She was way too young to be suffering this way.

Diabetes was winning slowly but surely. Years of alcohol abuse and neglecting her health were taking their toll.

One trip in particular proved to be healing in more ways than one, as Shannon, Tonya, and I met in Pensacola. That week we helped Mom clean, organize, and go through years of accumulated stuff. Mom had a hard time getting rid of things and she was trying to simplify her surroundings. It was obvious she was feeling a need to go through her belongings and designate where she desired things to go after her death. It was also during this trip she asked us to help her make funeral arrangements, "just in case something should happen," she said.

Mother's physical strength was going and her health was rapidly declining. It was important for her to make financial provisions for her funeral when the time came. So, supportively, we walked with her through a somber and trying process. The day we went to the funeral home was difficult. My sisters and I tried to be encouraging and helpful, but at best, the entire scenario was awkward and depressing.

"I think everyone should have the opportunity to make their own arrangements if something should happen to them. It not only takes a load off the family, but the person gets exactly what they want upon their death," I said. "Going through this with you is making me think about doing this for my sons. If something were to happen to me, everything would be taken care of the way I want it. It's not like you're planning to die anytime soon, you're just being smart," I babbled, trying desperately to ease the tension.

After meeting with the funeral director for a couple of hours so that Mother could plan exactly what kind of funeral and burial she wanted, he led us to a room with many different styles of coffins.

Mother was to "pick out" the coffin that best suited her taste. We tried to make light of the situation, cracking jokes as we walked around, as if we were shopping for a new car. But it was obvious mother was having a hard time; so were we.

I saw mother's eyes as she rounded the corner and saw the satin lined casket with pink roses embroidered. She stood there and stared, "I like this one. It's pretty" she said weakly. We all gathered around and chimed in, "Oh, Mom, it's beautiful!" As morbid as it may seem, there was a certain peace that came when she found it. It was the one. I thought, "It looks like you, Mama." Roses—she was a rose.

After all the paperwork had been signed and her final burial plans financially secured, we went back to the house. We tried to keep everything upbeat, and enjoy the evening together. We laughed, played some board games, and finally called it a night when it was very late. Around two in the morning I was awakened by Mother's cries. I opened my eyes and in the dark I could see her approaching my bed. Panicked and uncertain, I quickly sat up, trying to shake off the grogginess of deep sleep.

"Mom, are you okay? Are you feeling alright?" She couldn't speak for crying as she came to the side of the bed and knelt down beside me. "I'll go get Shannon and Tonya" I said as I quickly pulled back the covers thinking something must be wrong with her blood sugar.

"No, no. I need to tell you something." She was crying so hard she couldn't get her breath. My initial panic began to subside, but once again, I was lost inside my mother's turmoil, and almost like a well rehearsed queue, I found myself crying with her. Instinctively, I wanted to reach for the comfort of my sisters.

"Mom, let me get Shannon and Tonya."

"Give—me—just—a minute," she cried as she strained to breathe. I started stroking her.

"It's okay. Calm down," I whispered, knowing she was desperately trying to tell me something.

"Please forgive me," she moaned, as her emotional pain intensified.

"*What?*" I thought, trying to make sense of her disturbing plea.

"Forgive me for all those years—the things your daddy and I did. I'm so sorry, baby" she said, searching through her sorrow for the right words.

I interrupted her with my cries, "Its okay, Mama, it's okay. You don't have to…"

"No!" she snapped. "Let me finish." She paused to take a big breath. "You have to understand the way I grew up. It's not an excuse, but it's the truth." She began explaining the abuse her own mother endured as she witnessed it through a child's eyes. She talked about walking her daddy to the bar.

"For years its how I lived, and for years it's all I chose." She told me stories I would rather not have heard, but it was necessary for her to tell. After she finished, we embraced, and we cried. It was a healing moment for her. It was a healing moment for me. All the residue of the past washed away as our tears mingled together in the dark, releasing a lifetime of anguish and regret.

Peace filled the atmosphere, settling comfortably between us as I left her and returned to Atlanta; our unfinished business had been settled. It was only a couple of years later that we would get the call. In the early morning hours, a few days after Mother's Day that year, we received the news that Mother had died.

Mom was admitted to the hospital the weekend of Mother's Day. My sisters and I were going to leave to go down and take care of her, but she insisted that we wait.

"Let's see what the doctor says. I may need you more at home once they release me," she reasoned. She never made it home. She went into cardiac arrest in her sleep.

The funeral and burial took place just as she planned. When I saw her in the casket that she had chosen, my mind raced back to that week where everything had been resolved. I knew she was with Father God, and by His blessing, nothing remained unspoken. My mother's plea for forgiveness that night unlocked the peace that carried us through the grief of her home-going.

She was buried next to her little angel, Demedra, just as she wanted. At the graveside, my sisters and I sang *Amazing Grace*, a cappella, the way she loved to hear it. Once again, I am rendered speechless by the grace of God—the theme of my story and all of mankind. I am deeply grateful we did not have to wonder about Mom's eternal choice. It had been settled and we knew it. We spent the next few days going through mother's things, dispensing with them according to the wishes she had shared with us. Mom didn't have much of monetary value in this earth, but the greatest gift she left us was the peace of knowing she was with the Father.

A precious Jamaican woman in our congregation, that we fondly called Mother Rose, gave me a nicely framed poem after the funeral that I keep in the window of my kitchen to this day. It's entitled, *Remembrance* written by an anonymous author.

Remembrance

You can shed tears that she is gone,
Or you can smile because she has lived.
You can close your eyes
and pray that she'll come back,
or you can open your eyes
and see all she has left.
Your heart can be empty
because you can't see her,
or you can be full of
the love you shared.
You can turn your back on tomorrow
and live yesterday, or you
can be happy for tomorrow
because of yesterday.
You can remember her
and only that she's gone,
or you can cherish
her memory and let it live on.
You can cry and close your mind,
be empty and turn your back,
or you can do
what she'd want:
SMILE, OPEN YOUR EYES,
LOVE AND GO ON.

The poem was delicately framed against a
beautiful background; a peaceful deep blue sky
with a wisp of white clouds. A single rose adorned

the bottom of the verse. A rose—even now Mom's fragrance is with me, the bittersweet smell of both her wise and unwise choices.

History itself has taught us the power of our choices, and the consequences attached to them. An early history lesson exemplifies the power of choice through the lives of Abraham and Lot. When Abraham left his homeland to journey to the place God had called him, Lot chose to accompany him. They traveled from place to place until they came to Bethel, where they settled for a time. Both Abraham and Lot were materially wealthy, and they quickly outgrew the territory.

"Now Lot, who was moving about with Abram, also had flocks and herds and tents. But the land could not support them while they stayed together, for their possessions were so great that they were not able to stay together" (Genesis 13:5-6 NIV).

Fighting broke out between the herdsman of Lot and Abraham.

So Abram said to Lot, 'Let's not have any quarreling between you and me, or between your herdsmen and mine, for we are brothers. Is not the whole land before you? Let's part company. If you go to the left, I'll go to the right; if you go to the right, I'll go to the left" (Genesis 13:8-9 NIV).

Lot was to make a choice. It's important to note there is no record that Lot prayed before making a decision. There is no record of him seeking to hear from God in the matter. The scripture bears out, *"Lot looked up and saw that the whole plain of the Jordan was well watered, like the garden of the LORD, like the land of Egypt, toward Zoar. (This was before the LORD destroyed Sodom and Gomorrah.) So Lot* **chose for himself** *the whole plain of the Jordan and set out toward the east. The two men parted company"* (Genesis 13:10-11 NIV).

Lot made a selfish choice. He eventually moved his family to the city of Sodom, a wicked place. We see him in Genesis 19, sitting in the gate of the city, meaning "holding some political clout with the residents". He was very much a part of that wicked place, and that place became a wicked stronghold for his family. It was a place that would ultimately cost him everything.

Abraham chose to stay the course and follow God's plan for his life. *"The LORD said to Abram after Lot had parted from him, 'Lift up your eyes from where you are and look north and south, east and west. All the land that you see I will give to you and your offspring forever. I will make your offspring like the dust of the earth, so that if anyone could count the dust, then your offspring could be counted. Go, walk through the length and breadth of the land, for I am giving it to you.' So Abram moved his tents and went to live near the great trees of Mamre at Hebron, where he built an altar to the LORD"* (Genesis 13: 14-18 NIV).

Abraham listened for God's instructions and obeyed. His wise choice brought blessings that are still abounding toward the people of God today.

When the wrath of God visited Sodom and Gomorrah through fire and brimstone, the only influence Lot had was with his immediate family. His sons-in law remained in the city, not trusting the wise counsel of their father-in-law. Even as the angels were leading them out, Lot's wife made a terrible choice to look back, a spontaneous decision that proved fatal.

The consequences of Lot's selfish choice to take his family into Sodom cost him his wealth, his wife, his influence, the respect of his own daughters—and still God was merciful. He provided a mountain; a place of escape. What a picture of grace. Regardless of our choices, God has provided grace.

I often say, "life is a lesson, so take good notes." From both Abraham and Lot's choices, we are still reaping. At times, I reflect on what my parents lost due to their unwise, selfish choices. My father never knew his grandsons and my sons never had the chance to know their grandfather. My mother missed out on future weddings and births and our family still bears the marks of the choices made generations ago. I wonder how our family history might be different if my parents had followed their conscience on the night my father was murdered.

I can see the empty places that God intended for abundant life.

But I like what Augustine once said, "For those who love God everything works unto good; even sin." There is no such thing as wasted years with God. Every choice, wise or unwise, bears eternal value. Through God's design, we can't help but win. After all, *we are over-comers.*

CHAPTER SIXTEEN
THE TRUTH:

"Overcomers Live the Truth"

This is love for God: to obey his commands. And his commands are not burdensome, for everyone born of God overcomes the world. This is the victory that has overcome the world, even our faith. Who is it that overcomes the world? Only he who believes that Jesus is the Son of God.
I John 5:3-5 NIV

An unprecedented attack has been unleashed against our generation. The enemy is seeking to destroy God's people through mental torment, as never before. His greatest weapon in this war are the lies he continually feeds us. It is only after we recognize and expose the lies, that we can move away from a position of defeat to take our place as Overcomers. It has been my hope throughout this book to show how debilitating lies can be and how powerful truth is, when lived. A fiend of mine, Dr. Brian Adams says, "When you buy a lie you have purchased failure." What lie have you bought into that has kept you living in defeat? It's time for the church to live like Overcomers.

Overcomers walk in the truth and turn from the temptation to believe the lies

In the book of 1Kings, chapter 13, an anony-mous man of God travels from Judah to Bethel to confront King Jeroboam with a word from God. The king was in the midst of offering idolatrous sacrifices upon the altar when this man of God arrives, and begins to prophesy judgment. God uses the man in a powerful way to speak a bold word to Jeroboam. In anger, the king throws his hand up and points at this obedient servant and screams, "Seize him." (1 Kings 13:4 NIV). Immedi-ately the king's hand shrivels up and the altar is split apart.

Instantly the king recognizes he is not fighting a man, but the word of God manifesting through God's servant; his attitude makes an abrupt change. He begins to plead with the man of God to pray for him that he might be healed. God used this servant once again in a powerful way to ren-der a healing miracle to Jeroboam. The king urges him to come home and eat with him. No doubt it was an honor to eat in the king's home. But God had given specific instructions to the man of God, in order to keep him safe and untainted by the corruption of the land.

But the man of God answered the king, "Even if you were to give me half your possessions, I would not go with you, nor would I eat bread or drink water here. For I was commanded by the word of the LORD: 'You must not eat bread or drink water or return by the way you came' "(1 Kings 13:8-9 NIV).

To eat with the king would be to fellowship with his idolatry. So, in obedience the man of God took another path toward home.

The sons of an old prophet that lived in the land of Israel witnessed what this man of God had done, and shared it with their father. The old prophet told his sons to saddle a donkey so he could go find the man. The old prophet finds the man of God sitting under an oak tree and invites him back to his house in Israel for dinner. The man of God was quick to let the old man know he was given strict instructions by God to not eat or drink in the territory, and to take another road back home. The old prophet says, *"I too am a prophet, as you are. And an angel said to me by the word of the LORD: 'Bring him back with you to your house so that he may eat bread and drink water' (But he was lying to him)"* (1 Kings 13:18 NIV).

No doubt the man of God was physically exhausted. Most likely, he'd been fasting and was probably feeling spiritually drained from his encounter with the king and a little wiped out from the exertion of traveling. Often after being greatly used by God under the anointing, like this man, the body feels the release and the flesh suffers deep fatigue. We can find ourselves vulnerable at these times, and more easily fall prey to the lies of the enemy.

It's interesting that the old prophet claims an angel of the Lord spoke this contradiction. Some believe a deceiving spirit spoke to the prophet. Others think the old man, for selfish and possibly nosey reasons, made the lie up. Regardless of how the lie came forth, it was in absolute opposition to what the Lord had spoken. Paul warns us of falling into the trap of deception.

"*And no wonder, for satan himself masquerades as an angel of light. It is not surprising, then, if his servants masquerade as servants of righteousness. Their end will be what their actions deserve*" (2 Corinthians 11:14-15 NIV).

Even if someone comes along proclaiming a supernatural experience, if it is in direct contradiction to God's word, it is not to be followed.

Sadly, in his weakened state, the man of God did not resist the temptation and fell for the lie. After all, he seemed legit. The old prophet didn't offer any kind of reward and the fact that he was older most likely brought about a certain amount of respect from the man of God. He returns with the old man to his home, and as they are sitting at the table enjoying their meal, the true word of the Lord comes to the old prophet.

"*This is what the LORD says: 'You have defied the word of the LORD and have not kept the command the LORD your God gave you. You came back and ate bread and drank water in the place where he told you not to eat or drink. Therefore your body will not be buried in the tomb of your fathers'*" (1 Kings 13:21-22 NIV).

The man of God learned a hard lesson and suffered dire consequences for departing from God's instructions. God never contradicts His word. As a result, when the man of God departed, he was attacked by a lion on the road.

"As he went on his way, a lion met him on the road and killed him, and his body was thrown down on the road, with both the donkey and the lion standing beside it. Some people who passed by saw the body thrown down there, with the lion standing beside the body, and they went and reported it in the city where the old prophet lived." (1 Kings 13:24-25 NIV).

It would appear the lion had one single mission; to kill the man of God. The lion didn't devour the man's donkey nor did he attack the people who walked by, but stood beside the dead body on the road. Believing a lie brought about the man of God's demise.

Scripture compares satan to a roaring lion looking for someone to devour (1 Peter5:8). Overcomers understand this, and are diligent in truth. There will be countless temptations, throughout our Christian walk, to believe the lies the enemy conjures up. He'll tell you, *"You'll never amount to anything. God didn't call you. You're all alone. Who do you think you are? God won't heal you. Nobody loves you."* We must resist the temptation to believe the kind of lies our enemy sends our way, knowing that God's truth will disarm the lion.

"God is not a man, that he should lie, nor a son of man, that he should change his mind. Does he speak and then not act? Does he promise and not fulfill?" (Numbers 23:19 NIV).

Overcomers make daily decisions to live in truth.

The mindset of an Overcomer is something that is developed as we consistently walk in truth and are conformed into the likeness of God's Son (Romans 8:29). In the book of James we find the author writing to the Jewish Christians. In chapter 1, he equates double-mindedness to the tossing of waves by the wind. (v.6). Adam Clarke's commentary states double-mindedness could be compared to a man with two souls, who has one for earth and another for heaven; who wishes to secure both worlds.[6] John Wesley said, "A double-minded man—who has, as it were, two souls; whose heart is not simply given up to God is unstable—being without the true wisdom, perpetually disagrees both with himself and others.

In our years of pastoring, I have dealt with many double-minded believers. Depending on the day you catch them, they may or may not resemble an Overcomer. James said the double-minded man is unstable in all his ways (v. 8). How

6   http://www.godrules.net/library/clarke/clarkejam1.htm

true this is. I've observed they are often indecisive, allowing the current circumstances of life to dictate their mindset. If things are going well they are confident in God, and secure in what they believe. If adverse situations arise, they agree with the adversity and fall into discouragement. They are also easily misled. Because they are prone to doubt, it doesn't take much buffeting to cause them to question or forsake truth and buy into a lie. Another characteristic of a double-minded person is inconsistency.

In verse 2, James encourages the believer to maintain their joy no matter what test or trial comes their way. *"Consider it pure joy, my brothers, whenever you face trials of many kinds."* He goes on to exhort the believer to see the big picture. Understand that trials have a purpose, and good things are produced as a result. This is how we remain consistent in times of testing. Herein marks the life of an Overcomer.

Each day we have the opportunity to embrace the "overcoming" life. By daily bible reading, bible study, prayer, meditation, fellowship with believers and placing ourselves in a position of accountability, we fortify our faith and shut the door to wishy-washy living.

Overcomers know the difference between getting knocked down and getting knocked out.

Have you met people whose life circumstances knocked them down, but they got right back up? When looking for an example, I think of Beth, a wonderful woman who suffered through the pain of divorce. Beth had every right to be bitter. She was betrayed and rejected. She had given her life to God's work and married a minister. After standing by his side for many years, he chose to have an affair with her best friend. When I met Beth, I was amazed at her positive attitude. I wondered if she might be in denial. I was concerned that once the full impact of what happened to her hit home, she would fall apart. I decided I would be there for her, to help pick up the pieces.

I was surprised. Time moved forward and Beth still maintained her positive spirit. I never heard her speak an evil word about her ex-husband. She talked often about how good God was and how He was taking care of her, although she had lost almost everything. She remained consistent in faith, and her trust in God only grew stronger. God rewarded this precious woman with a godly man and I was honored to witness and participate in their wedding. Beth is an Overcomer!

Michael is another glowing example. This young man made some bad choices in his teen years. His mother often called, very concerned for him and we would pray together. Michael surrounded him-self with other kids that were into drugs and alcohol. They started committing petty crimes that led to a major and costly mistake.

One night he and his friends were driving around looking for trouble. Michael was in the backseat of the vehicle. One of the guys in the car pulled out a gun and randomly shot a man walking on the street. It was a drive-by shooting and Michael was guilty by association. Although he had not pulled the trigger, because he was in the car, he received a ten-year sentence in prison. His mother was devastated.

Michael was only nineteen years old. He was so remorseful that he cried in anguish when my husband went to visit, wishing he could take it all back. Prison was very difficult for him, but it was also the wake-up call he needed; he gave his life to Christ. Michael served his sentence and came out of the prison a better man. He didn't allow the situation to cause him bitterness. He learned from it, and changed his ways. He's a productive man with a wife and family, now living for the Lord. Michael's life example shows us the power of an Overcomer.

Hebrews, chapter 11, is crammed full of examples of people who were knocked down but never knocked out. Noah preached a message that was scorned, but he kept the faith and he and his family were preserved. Abraham suffered the blow of having to sacrifice his son, but he kept his faith and God provided a substitute to take

Isaac's place. Jacob was deceived by his father-in-law and feared his own brother; but he kept the faith and ultimately inherited the blessing. Joseph was hurt and rejected by his family, but he kept the faith and saw the restoration of his family, thus he became the agent of protection for an entire nation.

Then there was Samson (Judges 13-16). I often compare my father to Samson. Here was a man who was called by God, but he made some bad decisions that knocked him down. Samson experienced God's power in great measure. With a donkey's jawbone, he killed a thousand Philistines. He took hold of the doors of the city gate and tore them loose from their hinges and carried them to the top of a hill. He caught three hundred foxes and tied their tails together, and with a lit torch set the harvest fields of the Philistines on fire. He wreaked great havoc on the enemy, yet he struggled to conquer his flesh. In disobedience he gave the secret of his strength to the enemy. He was stripped of his power. His eyes were gouged out, stealing his vision. He was condemned to a life of slavery through forced labor. It would appear that he was down for the ten-count, but God was not finished with him. His missions had to be completed.

The enemy wanted to make a mockery of his life. Samson was brought out of the prison and taken to serve as entertainment at a Philistine party. They laughed at what had become of him. But as Samson stood between two pillars of the temple he cried, *"Let me die with the Philistines!" Then he pushed with all his might, and down came the temple on the rulers and all the people in it. Thus he killed many more when he died than while he lived"* (Judges 16:30 NIV).

Samson is listed as a hero in Hebrews, chapter 11. He refused to go down in defeat. He didn't stay down; he got back up and he completed his mission.

The enemy wants to make a mockery of all of our lives—just as he tried to do with James Jeter. My dad didn't stand behind a pulpit, but his life is still preaching a sermon. Maybe Dad's vision to reach souls was stolen from him, but his children and grandchildren are reaping a harvest of souls today. It would seem that daddy was stripped of dignity in the way he died, but like Samson, he has done more destruction upon the enemy through his death than he ever accomplished in his life. The enemy is defeated!

Hebrews 11 goes on to exhort us to get up and keep fighting.

And what more shall I say? I do not have time to tell about Gideon, Barak, Samson, Jephthah, David, Samuel and the prophets, who through faith conquered kingdoms, administered justice, and gained what was promised; who shut the mouths of lions, quenched the fury of the flames, and escaped the edge of the sword; whose weakness was turned to strength; and who became powerful in battle and routed foreign armies. Women received back their dead, raised to life again. Others were tortured and refused to be released, so that they might gain a better resurrection. Some faced jeers and flogging, while still others were chained and put in prison. They were stoned; they were sawed in two; they were put to death by the sword. They went about in sheepskins and goatskins, destitute, persecuted and mistreated—the world was not worthy of them. They wandered in deserts and mountains, and in caves and holes in the ground. These were all commended for their faith, yet none of them received what had been promised. God had planned something better for us so that only together with us would they be made perfect" (Hebrews 11:32-40 NIV).

Simply put, Overcomers are people of faith. Paul said it best, "I have fought the good fight, I have finished the race, I have kept the faith" (2 Timothy 4:7 NIV).

My Final Challenge

There is no doubt my parents loved us deeply. I have fond memories of their precious love. Times when my father would hold my hand while sitting on the couch, or put his arm around me and pull me close to him. Tender moments with Mother when she would stroke me and call me her baby.

Mom gave each of her girls titles that have stayed with us through all these years. She would say, "Shannon is my heart. Tonya is my heartbeat. Demedra is my angel. Jamie is my salvation. Myla is my comforter." We knew they loved us. They were good people that allowed bad decisions to destroy much of their lives. Friend, count the cost.

Jesus said, "And whosoever doth not bear his cross, and come after me, cannot be my disciple. For which of you, intending to build a tower, sitteth not down first, and counteth the cost, whether he have sufficient to finish it? Lest haply, after he hath laid the foundation, and is not able to finish it, all that behold it begin to mock him, Saying, This man began to build, and was not able to finish" (Luke 14:27-30 KJV).

By counting the cost of our decisions, we can avoid starting something we can't finish. God desires for us to finish well. He has given us everything we need to succeed. Even if you feel you've blown it, it's never too late. Get up! Start by making the right decisions today.

Are there patterns in your family that continue to speak defeat? Take your stand now and declare that the patterns of defeat are broken. Declare from this day forward that your family will reap the rewards of an Overcomer!

What kind of price tag can be put on a life? Friend, by choosing daily not to waste your life, but to invest it, you reflect the life God ransomed heaven to give you. Make today count. Make tomorrow count.

Help me give the devil a black eye. Rise up in faith and allow your journey to shout, "Overcomer!" Live it in truth and see it blossom into the victorious life God has promised you. Life is too short—*refuse to live a lie.*

Salvation Prayer

"Dear God,

I recognize that I have tried to live my life my way. My choices have brought me to a place of brokenness. I confess I have sinned against you. Please forgive me of my sin. Cleanse me of all unrighteousness. Jesus, I believe you died on the cross for my sins and you rose from the grave and are alive forevermore so that I might live also. I accept you as my Lord and Savior. Please take control. I surrender my life to you. In Jesus name I pray, Amen."

About The Author

Jamie and her husband, Victor, have been in full-time ministry, serving the Lord in Word and song since they got married. Pastors Victor and Jamie presently serve as the lead pastors of Life Church International in Duluth, Georgia.

Jamie has a Bachelor of Arts Degree in Christian Thought with an emphasis in Christian Counseling. She is an Ordained Minister with the Church of God in Cleveland, Tennessee. Jamie and Victor are the proud parents of two sons, Micah Andrew & Caleb Joshua.

Jamie has traveled throughout the world preaching the gospel of Jesus Christ in churches, at retreats, and in state, national, and international conferences. She has appeared several times on DayStar Television with hosts Marcus and Joni Lamb and many other network Christian programs.

One of her greatest joys is developing leaders through the nine-month Leadership Mentoring Program she has written entitled, "The Call To Mentor," her first published work. This popular leadership development tool has yielded great results in the local church. Above all else, she is first and foremost a passionate follower of Christ, as well as a devoted wife and caring mother.

Other Titles by Jamie Massey

55347093R00124

Made in the USA
Columbia, SC
16 April 2019